5 Secrets of Goal Setting

Creating your Action Plan
for getting the most from life

by
Dwayne Baptist

Press

5 Secrets of Goal Setting

Creating your Action Plan for getting the most from life

by
Dwayne Baptist

Published by Kokorozashi Press
Fredericksburg, VA

For more information, visit
5SecretsOfGoalSetting.com

Or contact info@5SecretsOfGoalSetting.com

For Ellen, the model student, muse, and wife.
with love always,

    db

Table of Contents

Acknowledgements

Developing a book on goal setting and achievement reminds you exactly how important it is to live the process you teach. One of my mentors, internationally renowned leadership expert Dr. John C. Maxwell, taught me a couple of key points that are so critical to developing a project like *5 Secrets of Goal Setting*:

- You need a team to succeed
- You are the message

Thank you, Paul Baptist, my coaching partner and son, for your invaluable help organizing and presenting this information.

Thank you, Ted Haenlein, Cara Parker, and Peter Baptist (#2 son) for your invaluable assistance as reader/reviewers.

Thank you, Donald Baptist, my father, for reviewing, for being a role model, and for introducing me to Jim Rohn and the entire subject of personal development and achievement.

Thank you, John Maxwell Team (JMT), founded by Paul Martinelli, Scott Fey, and of course, John Maxwell, for the inspiration to build my coaching business and to develop this book to add value to people's lives.

Thank you to the mentors at different points in my life, all of whom lived the things I teach in this book: Mike Nigro, John Crowe, and Larry Winters, and Robert Bruce

Thank you, Dexter Godfrey, for publishing your own book, *Fearless Success (It's Up to You): 45 Fearless Success Tips to Put into Action for Immediate Results*, which inspired me to develop this book from a workshop I delivered.

Developing this book reminded me that I need to live the lessons it teaches, being consistent so that people could see the message by the way I live. Fortunately, I had support in this area from the most consistent person in their winning habits: my wife Ellen—my muse and inspiration. To you, Sweetheart, I dedicate this book.

Prologue: Springing into Action

Setting and Achieving Goals Requires Focused ACTION

We all dream—of having more, of getting more, of being more. Even those few who have given up on the idea of "more" want to hang on to what they have. Yet in this time of economic uncertainty, we live in fear of losing it all. We wonder, "Is there a secret recipe that can help me be successful while avoiding loss and failure?"

An old Jewish proverb says that if you ask any two people in a room their opinion, you'll get three opinions. So it is with success. Everybody seems to have their own opinion on how to become successful, with people frequently having multiple confusing and conflicting ideas. Yet, classical sages such as Solomon and Napoleon Hill have discussed the fundamental concepts. Likewise, modern sages—including Jim Rohn, Tony Robbins, Stephen Covey, and John Maxwell—continue to share a simple success formula:

- Decide what you really want
- Create a burning desire to have it
- Make a plan, so that you know how to get there
- Carry it out with enthusiasm and abandon

It seems quite simple, doesn't it? But if it were easy, wouldn't we all be successful?

I am Dwayne Baptist, an executive coach. I help clients define what they want and become the people they need to be in order to achieve their goals and dreams. I want to share with you some things that I have learned through my own experiences and working with clients that will help you to spring into action, turning these concepts into action. **FOCUSED ACTION** is the key to achieving the success you seek.

> *FOCUSED ACTION is the key to achieving the success you seek.*

My success journey started at 15 when my parents took me to see Jim Rohn, a pioneer in personal development. Mr. Rohn encouraged me to develop and achieve my first written goal, to attend the United States Naval Academy. After attending the Naval Academy, I used these skills successfully while serving in the U.S. Marine Corps and continuing into a career in information technology and management consulting before embracing executive coaching.

Much as you might like it to be otherwise, you can't simply learn a formula and effortlessly become an overnight success. Much of what we think of as "learning" is the process of becoming aware and understanding a subject. To really learn something, we must do it. In fact, we must do it enough that we master it.

If practice is necessary in order to master concepts and truly learn something, then all success will naturally involve failure along the way. Falling short on a particular effort no more makes you a failure than completing just one makes you a success. Rather, success only comes from continuing to pursue our goals, even after a particular attempt fails.

Pursing Olympic Gold demonstrates this principle. Many talented children dream of winning it, but are they willing to do what it takes? Michael Phelps started swimming at age 7 — his sister was swimming, and his parents thought it would be a way for a hyperactive child to burn off energy. It turned out he had some talent, which was encouraged and nurtured.

The talented youngster maintained a rigorous training schedule, limiting his activities to school and swimming. Michael started winning local, then regional competitions. Soon he was a nationally ranked youth swimmer. As he continued to grow, he worked with his coach to set goals for greater achievement, eventually earning a spot on the 2000 US Olympic Team at the age of 15. He competed in 5 events at the Sydney Games, but only made it to the finals in one of those events—where he came in 5th. He failed at his goal of an Olympic medal.

Now, he could have given up there. A lot of elite athletes make it to one Olympics and never come back. Michael was determined to achieve his goals, however.

He continued training, competing internationally and qualifying for the 2004 Olympics. This time, the Athens crowds saw Michael win 8 medals—6 of them gold. His performance tied the record for the most number of medals earned by one individual in an Olympics.

Then came the iconic 2008 Olympics in Beijing. Again, Phelps competed and won in 8 events—becoming the athlete to win the most gold medals in a single Olympics. He finished his Olympic career at the 2012 Olympics in London; gathering 6 more medals and, with a total of 22, became the winningest Olympic athlete of all time.

Michael Phelps' success coming out of the 2000 Olympics was based on several factors. First, Michael focused on his dream. Everything he did was filtered through the lens of his goal. Second, Michael had developed a plan with his coach, so that he knew exactly what he needed to do each step of the way to follow through and win in 2004, 2008, and 2012. Third, Michael overcame the obstacles that got in the way. Significantly, when his coach Bob Bowman left Baltimore to accept the head swim coach position at the University of Michigan, Michael followed him and took classes so that he could continue his training.

GOALS for Success. Are you ready to make some of your dreams come true? We want to share with you five skills that will equip you to achieve them. The acrostic **GOALS** will help you remember them:

- **G:** **Getting Great Goals**
- **O:** **Overcoming You**
- **A:** **Achieving Alignment**
- **L:** **Learning and Adjusting**
- **S:** **Staying the Course**

Let's examine what we will explore in each part.

G: Getting Great Goals

You must know what you want and develop a burning desire in order to achieve those goals. Part 1 will show you a proven 5-step process for setting and achieving your goals. The process will help you get clear about what it is you are going to do and create a burning desire to achieve your goals.

O: Overcoming You

You must tame the two-headed monster, Fear and Procrastination, in order to keep moving and achieve your goals. Part 2 will show you how to face and defeat fear and procrastination. We will show you the secret that gets you focused, and enables you to take action in the face of internal obstacles.

A: Achieving Alignment

You must focus on the things that are truly important to you in order to maximize your activity and achieve your goals. Part 3 will show you how to figure out what is important to you, and how to align everything you do with your priorities. We will also show you why you should not do things that do not align with your priorities.

L: Learning and Adjusting

You must check your progress to make sure you are still headed towards your goals and to make the changes you need to get where you want to be. Part 4 will share with you questions you can ask yourself regularly to ensure that you stay on track with your goals. We will also show you how to gather and use the lessons you learn along the way.

S: Staying the Course

You must stay the course and keep taking action in order to achieve your goals. Part 5 will show you how to develop and define your burning desire. We will give you tools to turn obstacles into opportunities.

This book focuses on the fundamentals of goal setting and achievement. Jim Rohn said, *"Don't let your learning lead to knowledge. Let it lead to ACTION."* Advanced topics in personal development depend upon you mastering the fundamentals, which requires you to take action. This book will help you master the fundamentals so that you will be ready to learn and apply those advanced topics.

The five parts of the book are built so that you will learn about each principle from several angles, culminating in activities that will help you take action on your goals. In each section of the book, you will get:

- A case study to see the principles illustrated
- A discussion about why you need the principle
- An explanation on how the principle works
- An exercise to put the principle to work in your life
- A review to put the key points in one handy place

You can download a PDF workbook containing the worksheets that accompany the exercises to use at our website:

5SecretsofGoalSetting.com/Resources. If you register at the site you will also have access to other enrichment features I am preparing to support the book and an online community of others who are applying these principles to create their own success.

Now, let's begin the journey toward achieving your goals!

Part 1—G: Getting Great Goals

"Whatever the mind of man can conceive and believe,
it can achieve."
—*Napoleon Hill*

G: Getting Great Goals

O: Overcoming You

A: Achieving Alignment

L: Learning and Adjusting

S: Staying the Course

Chapter 1:   Always Faithful to Your Dreams

A Study in Setting and Resetting Goals

When you create an emotional connection with your goals and act on them, you unleash an unstoppable force. You might be thwarted in the short run, but relentlessly pursuing your dream will make it come true. I know this first hand. Let me share with you my first experience with the power of setting and resetting goals.

The 1960s were an exciting time to be a kid. President John F. Kennedy challenged America to land a man on the Moon by the end of the decade, and space mania was in the air. Like many kids of this era, I wanted to be an astronaut when I grew up.

As I watched the space missions, I noticed that astronauts tended to be military officers: Commander Alan Shepherd, Major John Glenn, Colonel Gus Grissom. I decided I wanted to join the military and embark on the path to becoming an astronaut.

Now the question was, which branch of the service? The 8-year old me considered the choices:

- The Army had no pilots at the time, at least in the space program.
- You could fly in the Air Force, naturally, but what could you do if you didn't fly? Fix airplanes?
- In the Navy you could fly or sail on ships and see the world.
- But in the Marine Corps, you could fly, sail on ships

(like the Navy), and even drive tanks or do other things the Army could do.

The choice was obvious to an 8-year old: who wouldn't want to be a Marine?

In the 8th grade, I had to write a paper on a career choice. I often got motion sickness and realized that made being a pilot and astronaut a bad fit, but I did want to serve my country. Therefore I researched how to become a Marine Corps officer. I learned that the Marines are part of the Department of the Navy. As such, Marine officers could be commissioned by attending the United States Naval Academy in Annapolis, Maryland. I understood that if you wanted to be a great doctor, you would want to go the best possible medical school to prepare. Therefore, if I wanted to be the best Marine officer, the Naval Academy was my destination.

Dreams are daydreams if you don't act upon them. I discovered this when my parents took my brothers and me to see the late Jim Rohn, a popular personal development speaker, when I was 15. Mr. Rohn's folksy talk was two hours of pure wisdom. He laid down a simple but powerful formula for getting what you wanted:

- Write down your goal.
- Create a burning desire.
- Figure out how to get it done.
- Remove all the excuses and obstacles that get in the way and take action.

I wrote down my first goal: *I will go to the U.S. Naval Academy and become a Marine Officer*. The good news was that I already had a burning desire and I basically knew what needed to be done because of my career project. I needed to remove all excuses and obstacles and take action. Studying everything I could about getting accepted to the Naval Academy, I discovered that at nearby Moffett Field Naval Air Station was the office of the West Coast Regional Director of Admissions for the US Naval Academy, Mr. Tom Teshara. I rode my bike out to meet him and established what would prove to be a productive relationship. Mr. Teshara appreciated my enthusiasm and politely put up with my quarterly visits.

As my senior year of high school approached, I applied to my congressman and received the required nomination. While I was feeling pretty good about things, I knew that if my plan had a flaw it was that I had been a lazy student. I had a lot of As, but also tended to get Cs when classes did not interest me. Afraid that my grades might not be competitive, I enlisted in the Navy's nuclear power program, with a start date following high school graduation.

Why did I choose the Navy if I wanted to be a Marine? Because the Navy's nuclear power school was the most academically challenging training offered in any of the armed forces. I knew that if I could demonstrate my academic ability I could make it in on a second try. Sure, I could have chosen to go to college for a year and retry, but I thought that it would be better to learn all I could about the life and men I might lead one day.

In my senior year of high school, I was one of 2,500 finalists qualified for an appointment to the Naval Academy. Unfortunately, only 1,400 could be offered appointments, and I missed the cut. I would have to reset my goal and try again.

Mr. Teshara suggested a route: attending the Naval Academy Prep School. Unfortunately, at 18 years old, I figured I knew better about what I needed to do than a 50-year-old man with 25 years of experience in the admissions process. I declined Mr. Teshara's offer and reported for boot camp.

My enlisted experience truly was an eye-opener for me. I met many other young men like me who had also wanted to go to the Naval Academy, but failed and had enlisted instead. The others thought that they had missed their one big chance and had given up. I also discovered that just because you want to do something does not mean that others want to help you. People want to put others in a box or category and leave them there. This should not have surprised me—they had plans and goals they wanted to achieve, and they needed the certainty that categorizing others brings. Consequently, I had to fight to earn the opportunity to reapply to the Naval Academy.

One example of the several obstacles I overcame, involved the Nuclear Power School's Command Career Counselor, a Senior Chief Petty Officer (a "Chief"), who refused to process my application. I pointed out to him

> *When you get clear about what you want, you will be able to achieve it despite the obstacles you encounter.*

that he did not have the right to deny my request—which was exclusively the commanding officer's prerogative. He could only *recommend* disapproval. The Chief was not pleased, and proceeded to "instruct" me on my duties and his prerogatives, at the top of his lungs. The Commanding Officer, Captain Brad Mooney, happened by, and was wondering what had gotten his Chief so worked up.

When Captain Mooney heard the situation, he told the Chief to have me in his office three days later to discuss my unusual request. Arriving at the appointed hour, I was seated in front of the Captain's desk. He asked me about my request. I explained my dream of going to the Naval Academy and having a career in the service. I explained to him the challenges I had encountered up to that point and how I was determined to succeed. It turned out that Captain Mooney wanted to see if I was a good sailor and had the courage of my convictions. As it turned out, he was a Naval Academy graduate and wanted to see promising, determined young sailors earn the opportunity. Based on my academic record and the interview, Captain Mooney approved my request. Shortly thereafter, I received a nomination from the Secretary of the Navy and was accepted to the Naval Academy.

My time at the academy was similarly fraught with challenges and obstacles that had to be overcome. I eventually earned a commission in the Marine Corps. I was able to serve my country, and the entire experience prepared me for a remarkable career in information technology and management consulting following my time in the Marine Corps.

My boyhood daydream was converted into a goal because I wrote it down, figured out what needed to be done, and then took ACTION until I achieved the outcome I wanted. When you decide and get clear about what you want, you will be able to achieve it despite the obstacles you encounter.

Chapter 2:   Being SMART about Goals

How to Set Goals You Really Will Achieve

Goals are the building blocks of all success in life. Well-developed goals focus values and priorities, moving you forward towards your definition of success. They act as a yardstick to measure the evolving situation, allowing you to recognize opportunities and distractions. In this way, goals help you reduce the confusion in your life.

Goals are a way to communicate with others, bringing them to your cause. Few things in life are done by individuals acting alone. Michael Phelps could not have achieved to his fullest potential without his coach, Bob Bowman, and support of his family and sponsors; several of his medals were for team relays. When you can clearly articulate your goals and your resolve, you give people the opportunity to buy into what you are doing, perhaps gaining valuable allies in the process. My journey to the Naval Academy required the help of many people, including Mr. Teshara and Captain Mooney. My resolve to overcome all obstacles to achieving that paramount goal, demonstrated by my actions, attracted them to my cause.

Clear goals allow us to share plans and express our values, allowing others the opportunity to buy into our plans. If we are not clear and excited, we cannot be compelling. Expressing goals clearly to others is the route to their support—the help that we will need to get the job done.

People often equate goal achievement with success, but this

is simplistic. Author and speaker Earl Nightingale said, "*Success is a progressive realization of a worthwhile goal or objective.*" It is sustained effort—ACTION—that makes people successful. The outcome is secondary because a successful outcome will eventually come from focused, sustained action. My initial efforts in pursuit of the Naval Academy led to failure, yet I was successful because I remained in the process and learned from that attempt. I developed new plans and tried again. Sometimes circumstances will require you to change a major goal. But, refocusing your efforts based on your values can lead to achieving even great things in the end.

What kind of goals should you set? Start by thinking about what you want: "*I want to lose weight.*" "*I want a new house.*" "*I want $100,000 in the bank.*" "*I want to climb Mt. Everest.*" But just how useful are these ideas, in terms of helping you get them? They are little more than a daydream stated this way.

Any goal must be a SMART goal to be useful and worthwhile.

SMART stands for:

- Specific
- Measureable
- Attainable
- Relevant
- Timely

Specific. Goals need to be specific to provide clarity regarding what you want. Many of people have set the goal "*I want to lose weight*", but they never get around to losing weight because they have not given themselves a specific instruction. Any amount of weight lost could satisfy this goal, whether it is one pound or 100. There is not enough substance to motivate them to action. Set a specific goal by being precise about what you want: "*I want to lose 35 pounds.*"

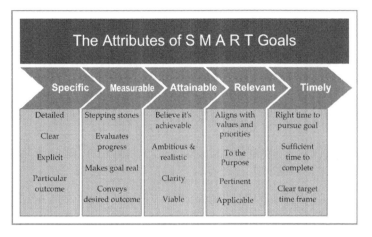

The Attributes of S M A R T Goals

Specific	Measurable	Attainable	Relevant	Timely
Detailed	Stepping stones	Believe it's achievable	Aligns with values and priorities	Right time to pursue goal
Clear	Evaluates progress	Ambitious & realistic	To the Purpose	Sufficient time to complete
Explicit	Makes goal real			
Particular outcome	Conveys desired outcome	Clarity	Pertinent	Clear target time frame
		Viable	Applicable	

How you state goals is also important. People get the best results when they focus on what they want rather than what they don't want. Everyone wants to be healthier, wealthier, and wiser. Everyone wants abundance and wishes to avoid sickness, poverty, and ignorance. If wanting the general concept were enough, everyone would already have these things. So, state exactly what you really want. Stating what you want makes you goals specific. *"I want to weigh 165 pounds"* is a much more specific, positive goal than wanting to lose 35 pounds.

Measureable. To achieve a goal, there must be a way of knowing that you are making progress. Specific and measureable are often intertwined, especially with simpler goals, as the means of being specific often involves something that can be counted or compared to a standard. In the case of losing weight, it's easy to tell: you can stand on the scale. If you know what you started at, you can set a schedule to see if you are making progress. You will also be able to tell exactly when you've lost 35 pounds.

Some goals can be specific without having a measureable component built in. For example, say you set a goal to climb

Mt. Everest—which is more specific than a simple goal to go mountain climbing. It would be silly to measure the progress of this goal by the elevation you are at until the very last stage of your goal, because there is so much more required to achieve this goal than simply scaling a peak. With this type goal, you need to create measureable components by creating lists of tasks to be done, setting dates, or identifying milestones along the way that help you determine the progress you are making towards achieving your goal.

Attainable. Deciding what is attainable can be a tricky matter. It is largely determined by what you believe is possible. What is attainable for one person may be utterly impossible for another, on account of their level of belief. What makes a goal attainable? Many things contribute to it. Consider climbing Mt. Everest. The first thing you might think is *"I'm too _____ (fill in the blank) to do it."* Did you know that over 5000 people have summited Mt. Everest, most since 2000? A 13-year-old boy was one of them. So were an 80-year-old man and a 73-year-old woman. A blind man and one who had lost his foot has also summited. Clearly, belief is part of what is needed to make something attainable.

You might not know if a goal is attainable right now because you do not have enough information. Getting the necessary permits to climb Mt. Everest can take 12 to 24 months. If your goal was to climb Mt. Everest a year from now, it might be difficult to achieve the goal in that timeframe. Could you be otherwise prepared within a year? The permitting schedule does not mean you cannot make the climb, only that you have chosen an inappropriate timeframe. What is more important to you? Making the climb or doing the climb in the next year? The answer to that question will help you decide if this goal is achievable. Most of my Navy buddies thought that going to the Naval Academy was unachievable for them because they were not accepted for the fall semester after high school graduation. Their real goal was to have something meaningful to do after high school. They succeeded. My goal was to attend the Naval Academy. Failing to go on the first try did not mean it was unachievable; it just meant I needed to find another way.

> *Failing on the first try does not mean a goal is unachievable. It means you need to find another way.*

Certainly, resources and a team matter when pursuing big goals. If you discover that your approach is not attainable, evaluate what are your real motives so that you can decide how to revise your goal and change your plan. Be very honest with yourself. Changing plans will often mean having to change yourself in the process. Consider the price you personally are being called to pay to achieve your goal and reaffirm you are willing to pay it. Do you need to learn a skill in order to succeed? Change a belief? Submit your ego and defer to another who is better able than you in some area? Are you willing to do this? Your willingness to pay the price will often be the key to determining just how attainable is your goal.

Relevant. There are many things you can do, but in the end what you do is a reflection of your priorities in life. I am not a fisherman, but when my boys were young, they were curious about fishing and kept asking me about it. I mentioned it to Joe, a colleague, who turned out to be a real fishing enthusiast. We made a date to go fishing with the boys. The day began at a sporting goods shop. Joe helped us buy poles and tackle. Then he took us to his favorite spot to fish from shore and we spent 4 hours casting and chatting, having a great time. It is a memory we made that the boys still talk about. Fishing was not relevant to me, but it was very relevant to Joe.

It was that relevance that made the trip (and memories) possible.

As with the fishing example, there are probably things in your life that you might enjoy doing but you cannot seem to begin. On the other hand, you might have no problem getting even very distasteful things done at work. Why? Because you have attached high relevance to the tasks at work because you have a strong attachment to the paycheck you receive. People with a strong sense of their priorities and values find it much easier to find the relevance of the goals they pursue. Conversely, they are also quick to avoid goals that are not relevant to them, whether a personal daydream, or somebody else's priority.

In cases where your goal involves adding something to your life that wasn't there before—such as the Mt. Everest example, if you are not already a mountaineer—it's important to work elements of your goal into your daily routine to establish an emotional connection with it. Ways of doing this might include building a training regimen to practice new skills daily, or researching elements of your goal.

Timely. There are two aspects to being timely with your goal:

- Is this the right time to pursue this goal?
- Do I know when I plan to complete this goal?

Farmers recognize that their occupation is a year-round proposition. While it might appear that they get the winter off because they aren't growing anything, it is actually a time for planning, maintenance, and preparation for the next season. The farmer who waits for the official start of spring to begin work risks being very late planting, which could lead to a reduced yield or even a missed harvest. Farmers recognize that they must be doing what is appropriate to the season if they are going to achieve their goals and have success on the farm.

While your goals might not be dependent upon the weather and cycle of the solar seasons, there is still a time and season to accomplish everything. Are you considering a goal that requires you to gain a skill so you can achieve it? Then before the season of doing will come a season of preparation. When it is the season of action, be prepared to put everything you have into achievement. The farmer who works hard all year long but does not work especially hard at harvest time will have little to sell at market if the crop rots in the field.

Understanding when you need to complete a goal will also help you understand timeliness. Goals that we perceive as easily accomplished within the timeframe we give them may lose their sense of urgency. An installment of "Foxtrot," a comic by Bill Amend I saw once around New Year's, perfectly illustrates this point (paraphrased):

Husband:	Do we have rice cakes?
Wife:	I don't think so. Why?
Husband:	My New Year's resolution is to lose weight
Wife:	It's December 30th. Why are you in such a hurry to start now?
Husband:	Not next year's resolution, this year's. I need to lose 15 pounds by tomorrow! It's a point of honor!
Wife:	(thinking) I thought your resolution was to lose 5 pounds this year?
Husband:	As it happens, I gained 10.

When people set a goal that they believe they can complete at any time, they do not establish a sense of urgency regarding its completion. They run the risk of being like that husband, setting the bar so low that they trip over it, causing themselves embarrassment. Often, they reproach themselves because of their failure. Avoid this problem by ensuring that your goals are set to be performed in the proper season and that they will be time-focused in a way that creates a sense of urgency for you.

Creating SMART goals challenges you, but also increases the likelihood that you will achieve them. Defining and writing your SMART goals, whatever size they might be, gives you the confidence to tackle other goals, and prepares you to tackle the great challenges in store for you in your life.

Chapter 3: Creating Goals You Will Be Excited to Achieve

A 5-Step Goal Setting Process to Bring Focus to Your Goals

You set goals because you want something more. You might want to have something. Maybe you want to make a mark on the world. Maybe you want to make a difference for your family. If all it took to achieve a goal was to decide upon it, then everyone would have everything they chose. If you look around you, you know that isn't the case. So, there must be something more to the process of achieving goals than deciding you want them. It takes three elements:

- Deciding what you want
- Make an emotional connection with the outcome
- Taking all the action necessary to see the job through to completion

Many people are willing to decide what they want. And many are willing to do the work needed to have their dreams. The problem most have in achieving their major goals is that they have not formed a strong emotional connection to their goal.

The secret to achieving your goals is to be very clear about what you want and why you want it, and then keep that information constantly in front of you until you achieve your goal. There is a formula you can use in order to set your goal and keep it in front of you. If you follow this process, you will be amazed at the power that is brought to bear—the pleasure created by setting and achieving your goals.

The 5-Step Goal Setting Process is very simple and straight-forward:

1. Set a SMART goal.
2. Develop a vision—a picture of the goal, achieved.
3. Decide the price you will pay.
4. Outline your plan.
5. Study your goal daily.

Chapter 4 contains tools you can use to support this process and explains specifically how to use them. For now, let's look at the five steps and understand their power.

Set a SMART Goal. Setting a measureable goal involves the SMART method discussed in the previous chapter. Remember to cover all five components: Specific, Measurable, Achievable, Relevant, and Timely. Further, make sure it is as clearly and simply stated as possible. Even complex goals can be stated simply. As you work through the 5-Step Process you will be adding details and layers that will create an emotional tie to your goal, which will be triggered by the thought of your simply stated, well defined goal.

Develop a Vision. Have you thought about what it will be like to achieve your goal? Stop reading for a moment and consider your most important goal. Imagine you have just achieved it:

- What exactly was accomplished?
- How do you feel about it?
- Imagine you are being interviewed by a television crew about your recent success, what do you tell them?
- Why did you pursue this goal?
- Who benefits?
- To whom are your thankful because they helped you along the way?

Doesn't this feel great?

One of the amazing things about your mind is that if you believe you can accomplish something and you vividly imagine the outcome, you often get what you think about. This works for good or bad, which is why you should focus on a positive outcome for your goal. When Jim Carey was an up-and-coming comic in Los Angeles, he wanted to be a successful actor. He wrote himself a check for $10 million. In the memo line, he wrote "For services as an actor" and postdated it by 5 years. He carried that check in his wallet, taking it out and looking at it often. He found a way to visualize his success and the rewards he hoped to get.

> *The secret to achieving your goals is to be very clear about what you want and why you want it, then keep that information constantly in front of you until you achieve your goal.*

Stating what you want is not "lying" or "science fiction". Architects imagine buildings in their minds before they ever draw the plans. Large buildings are never built without plans, so they must exist before the building can. Isn't your goal as important to you as a building is to an architect?

So, write down your vision of what it will be like when you have achieved your goal. Write in the past tense, as if you have already completed the task. When you review your vision, it will motivate your subconscious mind to find a way to ensure that your thought becomes reality.

Decide the Price You Will Pay. There will be a price you must pay to achieve your goal. It might be money—we're most familiar with that price, but there are others. You might have to change the way that you use your time. You might have to change a habit. You might have to build relationships with

people who can help you make your dream possible. Whatever the price is, it's important that you determine it accu-
rately, and that you decide that you are willing to pay that
price to have your goal.

When you understand what you will have pay to achieve
your goal, you will be able to evaluate it against your goal to
be sure that you are willing and able to pay the price, and that
your goal is in fact more valuable to you than the price you
will pay. Many cheerfully part with $4 and 15 to 30 minutes
of time daily for a cup of coffee because they feel it is worth
the price. If you needed $4 a day to achieve your goal, would
that be worth that cup of coffee? Would you be willing to
forego the coffee if you really needed that 30 minutes? The
answer may depend on how much you want your goal.

Outline Your Plan. Next, you need to do some basic planning to
determine how to achieve your goal. At this point you might
not know exactly how you will achieve the goal, but you can
put down the major steps you know you will need to take to
achieve your goal.

Dwight Eisenhower said, "Plans are worthless, but planning
is everything." Ike understood that few plans are ever exe-
cuted exactly as developed, so you should not be too tightly
tied to your plan. However, the exercise of planning helps
you understand what steps will be needed, the necessary resources, risks, and critical points in the process. The resulting
plan helps us understand the challenge we face, considers our
values and priorities, and identifies the gaps we need to address so that we can be successful. In the end, your plan will
be a useful yardstick with which you can measure progress,
evaluate the unexpected things that will happen, and make
adjustments to schedules and activities.

Eventually, you will need to get more detailed with your

plan. How detailed will depend upon your goal. Large, complex goals may need skilled teams of experts to help with planning and execution. But that does not matter for this step. The purpose of this plan is to firmly fix in your mind the key steps to achieving your goal. This way, you can keep it in front of you daily and create an emotional tie to your goal that will keep you making progress even when times are difficult.

A Chinese proverb says that the journey of a thousand miles begins with a single step. The final step in creating your initial plan is to determine something you can do today that can help you achieve your goal. If your goal was to climb Mt. Everest and you have never even been mountain climbing, then maybe your first goal would be to find a climbing gym in your area. By finding and accomplishing something that moves your goal forward today, you prove to yourself that you can take steps that can make your dream real. If you can take one small step, you can take another. Finding actions you can take daily to achieve your goal builds confidence and enthusiasm for your goal, helping you to achieve it.

Study Your Goals Daily. The way that you create a burning desire for your goal is to constantly keep it in front you. In the first four steps of the 5-Step Goal Setting Process you created an emotional vision and a plan for achieving your goal. Read this material at least twice daily. Keep it with you at all times so that you can review it when you have a momentary break in your routine. If you really want to increase your emotional connection, read your goal out loud or write it out at least once daily so that you involve more senses and trigger the subconscious to take notice of your words. This trigger will put the full weight of your subconscious to work on your goal. If you do this just before you sleep, fewer things will be competing for the subconscious' attention.

As you study your goals daily, one more thing you can do to strengthen your emotional attachment to your goal is to consider what you have to be grateful for because of your goal. You might be grateful for the opportunity to pursue the goal itself. You might be grateful for progress you have made, or for people that have helped you. As I will share with you in Chapter 9, gratitude is a powerful force that creates a strong motivation for action. Embrace it and see how excited you will become to achieve your goals.

> *Stating what you want is not "lying" or "science fiction." Architects imagine buildings in their minds before they ever draw the plans.*

Begin achieving your goals by setting SMART goals that you are emotionally motivated to achieve. But planning and motivation are only part of the equation. It is essential that you take ACTION in order to achieve your goals. The next several parts of the book will help you with that process. The next chapter will give you tools to move the 5 Step Goal Setting Process from ideas into action and get the results you want.

Chapter 4: Turning Ideas into Action - Goal Setting and Achievement

Time for You to Use the 5-Step Goal Setting Process

Are you ready to get clear on your goals and making the strong emotional connection you will need to achieve them? In this exercise, you will develop a goal using the 5-Step Goal Setting Process so that you can see how it works.

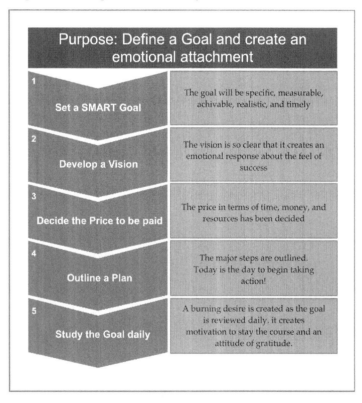

The worksheet in this section can be downloaded at the book's web site, http://5SecretsOfGoalSetting.com/Resources. This worksheet will allow you to keep your goal in front of you and will be portable enough to keep with you. While you can use the form right away, you might find it useful to use a scratch pad or whiteboard to gather your thoughts before putting the information into the form.

1. Set a SMART goal: Using the SMART questions to help you (found following the Goal Setting and Achievement Worksheet), develop a specific, measurable, achievable, relevant, and timely goal. Write your goal as though you already possess it. Write down the target date for achieving your goal

2. Develop a vision: Develop your clear picture of what the future looks like when you have achieved your goal. Make sure to:

Describe why you have achieved the goal, your motivation, and how you feel because you have accomplished it.

Write the vision from the point of view of the person who has just completed the goal. The work done to complete it is in the past. The benefits are now.

3. Decide the price to be paid: Determine what you are willing to do to make your goal a reality. This could be something directly related to the goal, such as time, talent, or treasure; it could be a skill you need to acquire or a behavior you need to change.

An optional step, list the things you are grateful for because you are pursuing this goal. You can also leave it blank to remind yourself to think about what you are grateful for daily.

4. Outline a plan: Outline the major steps you need to follow in order to achieve your goal. You don't need to have all your steps here, just the major ones that will remind you what needs to be done to stay on track and achieve your goals. Don't forget to determine what you can do today in order to start making your goal real. Now go do that step and start making your dream real.

5. Study the goal daily. Remember, the 5th step is to keep the worksheet with you and review it daily. Frequently reviewing and vividly imagining your goal achieved will motivate you to take action on your goal. Focused action is required to achieve your goal.

Goal Setting Worksheet

Goal	
Target Date	
Vision	
Price	
Gratitude	

Date	Plan Step	Completed

SMART Goal Questions

Specific

1. What do I want?

2. How do I want it?

3. When do I want it?

4. What are the details of my goal?

Measurable

1. How can I measure progress toward my dream?

2. In what ways can I quantify my achievements?

Attainable

1. What can I do to equip myself for the journey to achieving my goal?

2. What resources do I need to get started? To continue to make progress?

3. Who do I need to bring with me?

Relevant

1. Is this something I really care about?

2. Does this goal align with my ambitions?

3. How does this fit with my other goals and priorities?

Timely

1. What is the timeframe of my goal?

2. When must I get started?

3. What are the benchmarks for progress and the deadline for completion?

Chapter 5:   Review – Getting Great Goals

Key Points to Remember about Setting Goals

- The secret to achieving your goals is to be very clear about what you want and why you want it, and then keep that information constantly in front of you until you achieve your goal.

- Successful goals are SMART goals: Specific, Measureable, Attainable, Relevant, and Timely.

- The 5-Step Goal Setting Process for establishing and achieving your goals is:

  1. Set a measureable goal
  2. Develop a vision—a picture of the goal achieved
  3. Decide the price you will pay
  4. Outline the steps to accomplish the goal
  5. Read your goals daily

- When you create an emotional connection with your goals and act on them, you unleash an unstoppable force.

- When setting a goal, find something you can do immediately to start making your goal a reality.

- Dreams are just daydreams if you don't act upon them.

- When you decide and get clear about what you want, you will be able to achieve it despite the obstacles you encounter.

- When you can clearly articulate your goals and your resolve, you give people the opportunity to buy into what you are doing, perhaps gaining valuable allies in the process.

- Sometimes circumstances will require you to change a major goal. But, refocusing your efforts based on your values can lead to achieving even greater things in the end.

- Stating what you want is not "lying" or "science fiction". Architects imagine buildings in their minds before they ever draw the plans.

- Finding actions you can take daily to achieve your goal builds confidence and enthusiasm for your goal, helping you to achieve it.

- Planning and motivation are only part of the equation. It is essential that you take ACTION in order to achieve your goals.

Part 2—O: Overcoming You

"When you're worried, and you can't sleep, just
count your blessings instead of sheep."
—*Irving Berlin, White Christmas*

G: Getting Great Goals

O: Overcoming You

A: Achieving Alignment

L: Learning and Adjusting

S: Staying the Course

Chapter 6:   From Failure to Million-Dollar Man

Overcoming Fear and Procrastination to Enjoy Success and Freedom

The number one challenge you face on your success journey is **you**. As discussed in Part 1, you must develop an emotional connection – a burning desire – to achieve your goal. Life is going to challenge you with problems and distractions along the way, often leading to fear and procrastination. You must defeat them in order to achieve what you want. Allow me to share with you how one of my heroes, my father, dealt with his challenges and laid the foundation for a spectacular life.

Donald Baptist was facing a crisis. The 25-year-old husband and father of four was just a few days from being fired, right after the holiday season. He had given up a successful career in retail management to become a life insurance agent, and after six months he had almost nothing to show for it.

As a motivated 18-year-old husband and father he parlayed his after school part-time job at a San Francisco Bay chain shoe store into a full time job as the store's manager. He was so good at his job that shortly he was appointed the manager in charge of opening new stores in the chain. It was fun and exciting for a while, but moving every six months to open a new store was getting tiring. The money was quite good for a young man his age. But as he looked around he noticed his peers—the other store managers—were 10-15 years older than him. And in spite of their increased age, they were all making about what he was making. Don wanted more for his family and his dreams.

He realized that selling was a great way to make a living and control his life, so he began investigating other sales careers and settled on life insurance. It leveraged the selling skills he had been developing for several years. He thought that life insurance was a great product because it helped people protect themselves and their families, which he could feel good about.

Most important to him, however, was that life insurance was an opportunity to do the work once and be paid time and again, as a lot of insurance agents continue to receive commissions on premiums paid, even though the policy itself may have been purchased years before. So, through life insurance, he saw an opportunity to not only make a great income, but really build a great lifestyle.

Don was excited about the opportunity, but it was going to require him to learn a lot of new habits, and learning new habits is hard—especially when your family's livelihood is on the line. Pressure like that can make the process even more intimidating. The truth was that when Don got rolling he wasn't sure that he could succeed. Because he wasn't sure, he was reluctant to share his decision to move his life in a new direction with a lot of his friends and family.

This created a problem for Don, because the insurance business teaches people to start their career selling to their friends and family. Even if you don't successfully sell any policies, the practice that you get from learning in front of a sympathetic audience is necessary to help you develop the skills you need to succeed in the business. Selling insurance demonstrates the truth that you do and then you learn. Don needed to practice.

It was the day before the semi-annual sales meeting and awards banquet. Spouses were invited, but Don left his wife home because he didn't want her to see just how poorly he had done. As a matter of fact, he was certain that this was going to be his last day as an insurance agent.

At the banquet, Don watched as success was celebrated. When it came to the rookie category, he saw several guys who came in with him were achieving at the very top ranks of the agency. Their secret? They believed they were going to succeed and they followed the system laid out for new agents.

> When you beat fear and procrastination, you will be able to create the perfect life you want.

Yes, each had reservations getting started. But by following the plan and learning from each sales call, they mastered the fundamentals of the trade and had modest success. They proved the system worked.

Many in Don's situation might have nodded their heads knowingly and said that those other fellows were lucky, since they had made it while others had not. However, Don knew that he had not really done all that was asked of him. As he went home, he asked himself if he really wanted to succeed in the insurance business? Did he want all those things he thought were great about it? The ability to help people? The lifestyle? Did he believe that guys whom he thought were not as smart or talented as he was, yet managed to have early success, were really better than him?

In that moment of clarity, Don realized that he had not given the insurance business a chance. He also knew that he really wanted to have the opportunity to actually try the business and see if he could succeed. Further, he knew that in the morning he would be meeting with his general agent and would be dismissed if he could not provide a convincing reason why he should be given a second chance.

When he got home that night he sat down and did what he should have done six months before: he created a list of everybody he knew. He searched through yearbooks, Christmas lists, address books—anything that he could find that would help him remember who he knew and get in contact with them. He then developed a game plan to call the people on his list and set up appointments to share with them the good news that he was in the insurance business, and was able to help them to preserve their family's fortunes.

When he met with his general agent the next morning, he began by admitting that he had totally failed to follow through on what had been required of him. He acknowledged that the truth was he had been afraid, and that he hadn't really given the system a chance. Don then shared all of the work he had done the night before—the list, the plan, the preparation—and showed how he was finally ready to get started.

The general agent had decided before that meeting that he was going to fire Don. But when Don was open and honest about his accomplishments—and more importantly, his plans for the future—the gentleman decided to give Don 30 days more to demonstrate that he really was committed to the program and to his own success.

Did Don tear up the world in those first 30 days? No. Did he make progress? Absolutely. Over the next 30 days he sold more policies than he had in the entire six months prior, demonstrating that this process could work for Don Baptist.

Very quickly, as his skill grew by making more sales calls, Don saw his success rate skyrocket. By the end of the next six months—the end of the company's fiscal year—Don had earned admission to the President's Club, a program for top-ranked first-year agents. He was the number two new agent in the nation that year, selling over a million dollars in life insurance. Now, a million dollars in life insurance may not seem like all that much in the 21st century. This was back in the 1960s, however, when $10,000 was considered a large income. At that time, selling a million dollars in life insurance was a huge deal—and it only got better from there.

By overcoming himself—his fear and procrastination—Don developed his skills, eventually establishing a very successful financial planning practice that created an income and a lifestyle far surpassing the dreams he had hoped for, and enabling him to help many hundreds of people enjoy rich, rewarding lives and secure retirements. When you defeat fear and procrastination, you will be able to create the perfect life you want.

Chapter 7:   The Two-Headed Beast
The Challenges You Must Face to Reach Your Goals

Fear and Procrastination are the major reasons most people do not achieve their goals. Napoleon Hill, in *Think and Grow Rich*, said that there are 30 major causes for failure, but if you take a close look at that list you will see that virtually every one of those reasons ultimately has as its root cause either the fear of taking action or rebellion against plans.

We must address fear and procrastination if we are, in fact, going to have the necessary energy and willpower to get the job done. It is a vicious cycle because when people procrastinate (such as by putting off taking action on their goals) it leads to anxiety. When they start to get anxious about things, the human tendency is to focus on the things that they don't want, and that creates fear.

For example, suppose someone wanted to write a novel and their plan requires them to write one to two pages a day. Taking a week off—not because they are sick, but just because they did not feel like writing—will likely cause them to start feeling guilty. Most in that position start thinking about how it doesn't seem that they can finish the novel, which causes them to start to doubt themselves—they start to fear that maybe their big novel is doomed to remain in their head, never to be written down or shared with others. That fear begins to lead to inaction. Inaction leads to anxiety, starting an endless circle that keeps them inactive.

There are many causes of fear and procrastination, but fundamentally they revolve around six things:

- A lack of clarity
- A lack of skill or experience
- Boredom
- Stress
- Tolerations
- Distractions

A lack of clarity. Often, when people are not sure what they should be doing, they may slow down their pace or even stop taking any action whatsoever. Initially, they may reason that they do not want to make a mistake or interfere with another's prerogative. When these people do not go and find out what should be happening, slow-down and inactivity begin, starting the fear/procrastination cycle. Vague weight loss goals are an example of this challenge. If someone is not clear about how to create proper diet and exercise plans, they may never get started, or they may dabble, jumping from idea to idea, not sticking with anything long enough to determine if it will work for them.

A lack of skill or experience. Some people don't want to make a move unless they are absolutely certain they're not going to make a mistake. For example, I used to run a charity casino as part of an after-prom party organized in my community. Occasionally I had volunteers who wanted to help but steadfastly refused to play any of the table games. They were afraid that they would make a mistake dealing blackjack (our simplest and most popular game), causing a problem for the casino and the party. Most were satisfied when I told them to let the students know that they were new and that the students could earn $100 in casino money if they caught them making a mistake. But a few, though, were too afraid of being embarrassed by any mistakes, thereby limiting their ability to help us out.

Boredom. Part of the price of success is that it depends, in part, on performing a certain number of tedious things. Some of them are mind-numbingly boring, or so repetitive that people cringe at the thought of having to do them yet again. For example, people wanting a healthier lifestyle may face this at the gym. If they have only a couple of planned workouts, when they get bored and start making excuses for not going to the gym. Eventually they find something more interesting to fill the time, and their goal suffers.

> We must address fear and procrastination if we are going to have the energy and willpower to get the job done.

Stress. Major problems in our lives sap our energy, leading to fear and procrastination. When people struggle with challenges such as an illness, disharmony in the home, or trouble at work, it makes it difficult for them to perform in other areas. These situations sap their energy, making it difficult to act in other areas. Of course, procrastination and fear create their own stress, amplifying this problem.

Tolerations. There are things we tolerate in our life that cause stress and sap our energy, leading to fear and procrastination. Tolerations are things that we find ourselves working around because they are easier to avoid than to solve in the moment. However, ignoring them can have serious consequences. Have you ever seen an adult throw a tantrum over something, blowing it all out of proportion? They are reacting to something they have been tolerating in their life.

Distraction. Distractions can steal our energy and cause us to lose focus. For example, when it's a beautiful day outside and we see people enjoying life in the park across the street it's easy to start wishing that we could be in that park along with them, instead of sitting at our desk doing the work we need to do to be successful. Taking a few minutes to change our point of view can be beneficial, but regularly succumbing to the temptation of instant gratification will distract us from our goals.

The bottom line is that fear and procrastination rob us of the principal thing that we need in order to achieve our goals: ACTION. Finding ways to confront fear and procrastination will help us focus on identifying the right actions we need to take in order to achieve our goals.

Chapter 8:   Lifting the Veil on Procrastination

Secrets for Understanding and Fighting Procrastination

Everyone procrastinates, at least once in a while. When we realize it we feel guilty because we are putting off things we decided we needed to do. Internet entrepreneur and venture capitalist Paul Graham says that some of his most productive friends are the worst procrastinators he knows. He also points out that we procrastinate three different ways:

1.   Doing nothing instead of what we should be doing.
2.   Doing something that is less important than what we should be doing.
3.   Doing something more important than what we should be doing.

What? Doing something more important is procrastinating? Yes. Procrastinating is about avoiding something you know needs to be done. Sometimes we procrastinate out of a spirit of rebellion, other times from fear. But if we have decided now is the time to do something and we avoid it, we are procrastinating.

When we are working toward our goals, it is easy to think that our conscious, rational part is in control, guiding our daily actions. We are made of emotional, rational, and physical parts. Procrastination is our subconscious trying to tell us there is a conflict between our values and our activities. Maybe our subconscious is warning us that something is missing. Maybe our emotional and physical parts are rebelling, rejecting what the rational commands. In the end, these are clues that our values and priorities are somehow out of sync with the task at hand. Part 3 will deal extensively with the concept of aligning your values and goals. Strategies for proper alignment will help you to systematically avoid procrastinating. The strategies discussed here will help you to deal with the immediate problem of getting on track when you are procrastinating.

When procrastination strikes, take these steps to address the problem:

- Determine if you are procrastinating
- Determine what is really important to you
- Decide how to handle the moment
- Decide how to avoid this situation in the future

1. Determine If You Are Procrastinating. So, are you really procrastinating? There is a difference between taking a break and procrastinating, just as there is a difference between being busy and productively tackling our goals. When you realize that you are procrastinating, call a stop to everything, acknowledge your procrastination and then use the rest of this checklist to address the issue. This acknowledgement is not surrendering to the habit. Just as you cannot clean a house if you cannot see the dirt, you must accept responsibility and decide that you are going to change your situation. If you are not sure whether you are procrastinating, move to the next step. It will help you be clear about your motives.

2. Determine What is Really Important to You Right Now. Since procrastination is evidence that something is out of alignment between your values, priorities, and goals, you need to decide what is important to you at the moment. This is a time for candor with yourself. You value many things. Which is most important to you at any given time is a function of your awareness in the moment. For example, when I was a manager in a consulting company, I had to be careful when staff members came with job-related work challenges. My natural desire to be helpful and my pleasure in solving problems could easily get in the way of my higher values and priorities of developing my staff and dealing with larger company issues if I allowed it—at which point the distraction is procrastination.

It is easy to think that your highest priorities are always the most important things you could (or should) be doing. Sometimes people procrastinate because they are tired or feel a need to spend time with others (for example, family or friends). Get honest with yourself. If you need to rearrange your priorities, do so. If not, continue down this list.

3. Decide How to Handle the Moment. Once you understand your internal conflict, you can decide how to handle the moment. Here are several strategies my clients and I have used successfully to deal with procrastination in the moment:

- Take a break
- Focus on Your Priorities and Values
- Take Baby Steps
- Change your routine
- Reward yourself

Take a Break. As counterintuitive as this suggestion seems, sometimes the best way to get moving is to deliberately walk away from the task for a period of time. Marines on a long march stop for 10 minutes each hour. This short break allows individuals to adjust their equipment, grab a quick drink of water or a small snack, and relax from hauling a load that is often in excess of half their body weight. Individuals know that they will be able to take that break, so they are more inclined to keep to the task of marching without falling out of formation.

Giving yourself a chance to recharge and reorient can also help you keep to task without guilt. Of course, you can do other things in that break. Just be sure that these other activities do not sap additional energy. That would be procrastinating through avoidance. Suppose you need a longer break? Take the time you need. Just be sure that you are getting refreshed for your return to the task and not continuing to avoid it.

What if you need a vacation? Then take a moment and schedule it. That alone can reassure your subconscious that the matter is being addressed and allow you to get back to work. The key is to be deliberate about your decision to rest and to honor it by recharging your batteries without guilt.

Focus on Your Priorities and Values. Sometimes all you need in order to get back to work is to reconnect to your priorities and values, and to relink them to pleasure rather than pain. Boxing great Muhammad Ali once said that he absolutely hated every minute that he worked out during his boxing career. He trained hard—face it, boxing is brutal. Practice must likewise be brutal. In the end, what kept him motivated was not the pain he was enduring, it was his vision of the joy and the pleasure that he was going to take in being the champion.

Take Baby Steps. Are you stuck because you don't know where to start? Perhaps the task is overwhelming? If that's the case, then start small by breaking the task down into something that you believe you can accomplish. The very act of completing a task, however small, will increase your confidence and build your belief that you can tackle more and bigger parts of your project in order to get it done.

This is one of the reasons why, in the 5-Step Goal Setting Process, you need to figure out some related action you can do to move that day on that goal. A small victory shows that you can make progress on your goal. It will also help you get perspective, even gain some clarity about your goal and the next steps you need to take to exploit the victory and gain momentum.

Change Your Routine. If you are struggling to get working because you cannot stand the thought of doing the chore in front of you, then perhaps what you need is a change of routine. Mix things up a little bit. For example, if you are at the gym and cannot get motivated doing your usual routine, change the order you do your exercises. Even better, find alternate exercises that will give you the same benefit but done in a different way.

If changing the order you do things isn't an option, then perhaps you can change the time you spend on different parts of your routine. For example, what if you usually pay bills by writing all the checks at once, then stuffing the envelopes, stamping them, and addressing them? Changing the routine to get one completely done, addressed, and stamped might help you feel as though you are making progress. Mixing it up will stimulate your mind and give you something that you can point to as an accomplishment in order to keep you moving forward.

Reward Yourself. Another strategy for getting yourself moving and focused on the right things is to reward yourself.

"Wait a second. Isn't that bribery?"

In a word: yes.

There isn't anything necessarily wrong with giving yourself rewards, if they are proportionate to the level of the accomplishment. If you are writing a novel, a $100-a-plate dinner to celebrate the one page you wrote today is counterproductive. But that does not mean you cannot find a suitable reward—

something enjoyable—which can be the motivation to get something done. Parents use rewards to train children to develop good habits. It will work for you as well when you find the thing you truly love.

For example, my wife Ellen relaxes by cross-stitching. When she has challenging work to do, she uses the opportunity to cross-stitch later in the day as a reward for tackling the tough chore. She is very good about not cross-stitching on days she does not get her key goal handled.

Rewards are especially effective when you need to break tasks down to baby steps. Small rewards (a handful of popcorn or a slice of orange) can be great motivators to keep you going until you have created the momentum you need to continue uninterrupted.

4. Decide How to Avoid the Situation in the Future. Sometimes people find themselves repeating procrastinating behaviors. When this happens, there is something in the environment that causes serial procrastination. Thomas Leonard, one of the founders of the life coaching movement, called these *tolerations* – things you tolerate, but which steal your energy in exchange. Tolerations are things that we find ourselves working around because they are easier to avoid than to solve in the moment. To overcome procrastination brought on by tolerations, you must deal with your tolerations.

Fundamentally, there are two ways to deal with tolerations: change your environment, or change your thinking. Deciding the right approach depends upon the nature of the toleration itself. For example, suppose you are really unhappy about your car. Why is that? One reason could be that it is in poor condition. Dealing with the car, either by making repairs or replacing the car will solve the problem.

Suppose that the car is fine mechanically, but it doesn't fit your image of the kind of car you should have. Maybe your rational self has always bought practical cars because the people you know believe that cars are transportation, period. But your secret desire is to have a sporty two-seater because it represents freedom and fun. What you have is a conflict of values. You need to examine why you hold the beliefs you have about cars and decide which value really is more important to you. (Part 3 will examine the alignment of values.) If practical transportation is your true value, then you should acknowledge this and just smile when someone talks about sports cars. It does not mean you will never have one, but that you can be happy knowing you are doing the thing that is more important to you for now. On the other hand, if freedom and fun are the higher values, then get the car you really want! That will end your internal conflict and you can concentrate on more important things.

> Tolerations – *things you tolerate, but which steal your energy in exchange*

Would you like to get that new car, but you cannot afford it? Then perhaps you have a conflict in priorities. Does the car have to be brand-new, or will a used car suffice? Can you see how this can challenge your values and priorities? Neither decision is intrinsically correct. However, given your values, priorities, and resources, only one choice is right for you. You might also have to consider whether buying a car is right for your resources now. If it isn't, then making a plan so that you can will help you handle the toleration.

The combinations and permutations are endless, based on what you value. The key to dealing with tolerations is to understand what you are tolerating, understand why it is a problem, and address the real problem. You do that by doing the appropriate thing:

- Make a change in your environment
- Clarify your values and priorities, acting on them
- Discovering a new way to see the issue so that it is no longer a problem
- Make a plan to solve a problem you cannot change right now

One of the exercises in Chapter 10 will help you begin to re-solve your tolerations.

Chapter 9:   Attitude or Gratitude?
How Gratitude Can Affect Your Attitude and Help You Succeed

Don's story in Chapter 6 demonstrated how critical attitude is to achieving whatever you want in life. We attract to us things just like ourselves. When Don was uncertain and unwilling to commit, others were uncertain and unwilling to commit to him. When he made the decision to change his attitude about the insurance business, his new positive attitude attracted clients and propelled him to be the number two rookie in the entire nation his first year in the insurance business. Did everyone become a client? No, but Don was no longer looking for those who did not want insurance. He looked for those who did.

What sort of attitude do you have? Why don't we take a quick little test? Read each question and pick the answer that resonates with you. Don't overthink it:

1. When a problem is encountered, do you

    a. Say, "Oh great. What next?"
    b. Get excited about the challenge that is being presented?

2. When something goes wrong, is your first thought,

    a. "How is this going to affect me?"
    b. "How do I tackle this challenge and solve the problem?"

Was your initial response "a" to each? If so, you are more concerned about how things affect you, rather than how you can affect things. While we are all interested in ourselves, people with a positive mental attitude understand that they are responsible for themselves—that they are not helpless bystanders. Dr. Viktor Frankl, Holocaust survivor, came to realize in the concentration camp that even though the Nazis could control his physical situation, they could not control his attitude. He summarized it this way: "Between stimulus and response there is a space. In that space is our power to choose our response. In our response lies our growth and our freedom." This is the essence of a positive attitude.

If you are interested in developing and strengthening a positive mental attitude, there are many great books on the subject, such as *The Power of Positive Thinking* by Norman Vincent Peale and *The Master Key to Riches* by Napoleon Hill. For now, understand that taking action with a positive mental attitude is critical to success. It is a key to beating fear and procrastination because it creates confidence in yourself and faith in your goals.

> *Between stimulus and response there is a space. In that space is our power to choose our response. In our response lies our growth and our freedom.*
>
> *--Viktor Frankl*

Have you ever wondered why you can be so sure and full of faith in one area of your life, yet still be terrified in other areas? Take, for example, a snowboarding champion who does amazing things on the slopes. Despite his physical courage, that king of the slopes may also be a shy young man, tongue-tied around the ladies. He has faith in his snowboarding skills because he has focus and takes action. Without focus and action on the social scene, however, he is shy.

Study after study shows that successful athletes visualize themselves (or mentally model) successfully performing their routines. They also use tools like "self-talk" to remind themselves about their model. Their self-talk also includes thoughts about the things they value and how it will feel to achieve their goals—similar to the information we record and read in the 5-Step Goal Setting Process.

Short of an epiphany such as Don had, how can you chase away fear when it challenges your plans? In the musical *White Christmas*, Bing Crosby croons,

"When you're worried and you can't sleep, just count your blessings instead of sheep, and you'll fall asleep counting your blessings."

I don't know about you, but counting sheep never worked for me. However, there is a case for counting blessings. Dr. Robert A. Emmons of the University of California, Davis, conducted research into gratitude and discovered those who kept a gratitude list were more positive and also more likely to be making progress on their personal goals.

Counting your blessings—being grateful for things—is a method of taking faith and putting it into action. I believe there is a distinction between thankfulness and gratitude. There are a lot of people that are thankful for people and things for a moment, but they are never motivated to action because of it. Consequently, the impact of the thankfulness is limited.

Do you appreciate your mother because she put up with you for all those years as a child? Maybe you are thankful for a teacher that opened your eyes and exposed you to a world that you've embraced and made your own in a powerful way. Have you ever told your mother that you appreciate what she did? Have you ever thanked that teacher? Don't waste a moment, let them know.

What if it is too late? You can still act. A few years back, my family mentioned that one of my high school teachers had passed away. I left a message for her family at a memorial web site they had set up for her. My words were a comfort to her family. What if even that isn't possible? Then decide to do something in that person's honor.

Andrew Carnegie was thankful for the opportunity that America provided a young Scottish immigrant who came to America as a teenager. After he passed away, his executors found a note in his desk he had written to himself. It was his goal, stating, "I will spend the first half of my life accumulating wealth, and I will spend the second half of my life giving it all away." Why did he do this? He was grateful to the United States for the opportunity it had provided him and he wanted to share his good fortune so that others might be inspired to do the same.

What are you grateful for? To whom are you grateful? Take action. Thank them.

Chapter 10: Turning Ideas into Action - Beating Fear and Procrastination

Exercises to Zap Tolerations and Catalog Your Blessings

The preceding two chapters are chock full of ideas on overcoming fear and procrastination, and they may all appear to be reactive to the situation, but there are actually some proactive things that we can do to help defeat fear and procrastination. I've prepared two exercises to help you take action and do something so that you can learn about overcoming fear and procrastination. You're going to start by zapping some of your tolerations, and then you'll create a gratitude journal. The worksheets are at:

5SecretsofGoalSetting.com/Resources.

Zapping Tolerations

This exercise has two phases. The steps for the two phases are shown in the graphic on the next page.

1. Create a List of 20. Using the sheet provided, list 20 things you are tolerating. As discussed in Chapter 8, Tolerations are anything you put up with in order to get other things done, but rob your energy. The sheet has five columns:

- A handy number to track the Tolerations
- A space to describe the Toleration (see step 1)
- E/A for designating the approach for addressing the Toleration (see step 2)
- A place to describe your solution (see step 3)
- Checkboxes to track progress (see step 4)

Once, in a seminar, a participant told me, "I've only got 3 tolerations!" When asked if that meant he had no pet peeves or problem clients, he laughed. When he thought about it, he realized that sixty percent of his time was consumed by just five percent of his clients. To add insult to injury, that five percent represented just three percent of his revenue. He realized that he was tolerating some bad customers. By eliminating that toleration, he was subsequently able to have more time to prospect new clients and more than replace that income lost with customers that appreciated what he could do for them.

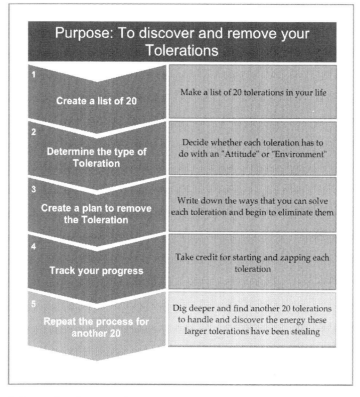

Purpose: To discover and remove your Tolerations	
1 Create a list of 20	Make a list of 20 tolerations in your life
2 Determine the type of Toleration	Decide whether each toleration has to do with an "Attitude" or "Environment"
3 Create a plan to remove the Toleration	Write down the ways that you can solve each toleration and begin to eliminate them
4 Track your progress	Take credit for starting and zapping each toleration
5 Repeat the process for another 20	Dig deeper and find another 20 tolerations to handle and discover the energy these larger tolerations have been stealing

2. Determine the type of Toleration. Tolerations are a matter of either your Environment or your Attitude. Understanding which will determine how you handle it. If you don't like where you live, but that is where the job you love, your toleration could be

- Environmental—I need to find a great place to live and change jobs to live a happier life; after all I can always find another great job.

- Attitude—My job is so awesome, but if I didn't live where I do, I wouldn't be blessed with such a great job.

The choice is yours. Do you see how understanding your values can help you decide which is the right course of action for you? The key is to consider which it really is so that you can create a plan accordingly.

3. Create a plan to remove the Toleration. You know what you need to do. Make your plans so you can take action and resolve the Toleration.

4. Track your progress. Did you create a plan? Great! Check the first block in the worksheet. When you complete your plan, Zap that Toleration by checking off the second box. Do you feel the energy surging back into you?

5. Repeat the process for another 20. The second phase is to repeat the first phase. I found that for many, handling the first 20 creates space for them to become more aware of the really big things that they are tolerating in their life—sometimes things so big that they do not recognize them as problems. Sometimes you get lucky, like my seminar participant, and discover a big toleration in the first 20, but why not take the time to really discover and eliminate the problem areas in your life?

I find that it is a good idea to return to this exercise once a year and see how toleration-free you can make your life.

Gratitude Journal

The worksheet provides you two versions of a Gratitude Journal starter list. The gratitude journal really is a simple thing to do. You can use one to add as many things as you like in a day. If you are someone who likes a sense of order and doing exactly what is asked, you might prefer the second sheet, which provides ample space to express gratitude for five things daily.

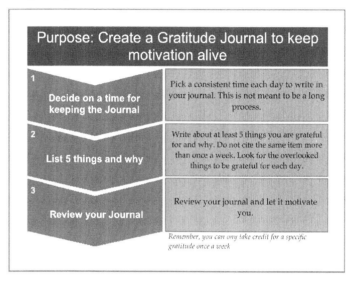

Purpose: Create a Gratitude Journal to keep motivation alive

1	Decide on a time for keeping the Journal	Pick a consistent time each day to write in your journal. This is not meant to be a long process.
2	List 5 things and why	Write about at least 5 things you are grateful for and why. Do not cite the same item more than once a week. Look for the overlooked things to be grateful for each day.
3	Review your Journal	Review your journal and let it motivate you.

Remember, you can ony take credit for a specific gratitude once a week

1. Decide on a time for keeping the journal. Keeping a gratitude journal is actually relatively simple. But to get the most from it you must be consistent, so pick a time and stick to it. You might consider journaling when you do the reviews we will discuss in Part 4.

2. List 5 things and why. When you think about it, there are many things you could be grateful about. For purposes of the exercise, pick at least 5 people or things for which you are grateful. Yes, some days might be more difficult than others. But the point of this exercise is to help you become aware of just how blessed you really are. Even on bad days, there are small consolations that can help you keep moving forward.

Of course, you can be grateful for certain things on a daily basis, but if your reason is the same daily, it can only count once a week. The point is to get you to consider additional dimensions of gratitude. For example, I look for reasons to be grateful for my wife Ellen daily. Here is a recent example of how I was grateful for her daily during a week:

- *Sunday:* she planned a great family event we enjoyed with our sons
- *Monday:* she advised me on a business challenge
- *Tuesday:* she works out hard to stay in shape and beautiful
- *Wednesday:* she took care of some business reports
- *Thursday:* we enjoyed time together having frozen yogurt at Menchie's
- *Friday:* she cleaned house, giving us a beautiful place to rest and relax together
- *Saturday:* I was grateful for her example as she shared a lesson from her personal meditation

3. Review your journal. It is fun to think about the great things you have to be thankful for, but don't let your appreciation for things keep you from taking action in response to these blessings. You are under no obligation to do anything about these blessings, but let them inspire you to do something in appreciation.

When you are discouraged, looking over your Gratitude Journal will also help you see the bigger picture and realize just how blessed you are. And, of course, "When you're worried, and you can't sleep, [you can] count your blessings instead of sheep and [you *will*] fall asleep, counting your blessings."

Zap Those Tolerations!

# Toleration	E / A	Solution	Plan / Zap
1			□ □
2			□ □
3			□ □
4			□ □
5			□ □
6			□ □
7			□ □
8			□ □
9			□ □
10			□ □
11			□ □
12			□ □
13			□ □
14			□ □
15			□ □
16			□ □
17			□ □
18			□ □
19			□ □
20			□ □

Gratitude Journal

Date	I am grateful for...	Because...

Gratitude Journal

Date	
I am grateful for...	**Because...**

Date	
I am grateful for...	**Because...**

Chapter 11:   Review - Overcoming You

Beating Fear and Procrastination

- Fear and Procrastination are the biggest reasons people do not achieve their goals.

- To beat fear, we must face it.

- Action cures fear.

- Procrastination is not all bad. Often, it is trying to tell us something about our values, our energy, or our focus.

- The four steps for dealing with procrastination are:
  1. Determine if you are procrastinating
  2. Determine what is really important to you
  3. Decide how to handle the moment
  4. Decide how to avoid this situation in the future

- There are things we tolerate in our life that cause stress to sap our energy. Dealing with these tolerations will give us more energy and confidence to act.

- You cannot clean a house if you do not see the dirt.

- Gratitude is faith in action.

- The number one challenge you face on your success journey is you.

- We must address fear and procrastination if we are, in fact, going to have the necessary energy and willpower to get the job done.

- The bottom line is that fear and procrastination rob

us of the principal thing that we need in order to achieve our goals: ACTION.

- Fundamentally, there are two ways to deal with tolerations: change your environment, or change your thinking.

- "Between stimulus and response there is a space. In that space is our power to choose our response. In our response lies our growth and our freedom."
  —Dr. Viktor Frankl

Part 3—A: Achieving Alignment

I would rather be ashes than dust!
I would rather that my spark should burn out in a
brilliant blaze than it should be stifled by dry-
rot.
I would rather be a superb meteor, every atom of me
in magnificent glow, than a sleepy and perma-
nent planet.
The function of man is to live, not to exist.
I shall not waste my days trying to prolong them.
I shall use my time.
—Jack London

G: Getting Great Goals

O: Overcoming You

A: Achieving Alignment

Chapter 12: A Picture is Worth a Thousand Words
Chapter 13: What You Value Gets Done
Chapter 14: Finding Your Diamonds
Chapter 15: Turning Ideas into Action - Values and
Ambitions
Chapter 16: Review - Achieving Alignment

L: Learning and Adjusting

S: Staying the Course

Chapter 12: A Picture is Worth a Thousand Words
A Story about Clarifying Values and Discovering Ambition

Are you ambitious? What values govern your life? The first two parts of the book focused on how to create a goal and deal with the challenges that can keep you from achieving it. But there are other enemies to achieving your goals. Many are frustrated because they do not have a clear goal to pursue. Those with goals can be frustrated if they do not have a clear direction, or burning ambition, to focus their energies. How you pursue your ambition is an expression of your value system (or "values" for short). Let me share a story about how my son, Paul, clarified his values and discovered his ambition.

Growing up, Paul was a big Japanese animation – Anime – fan. As he got more involved in the hobby, he found ways to get hold of titles direct from Japan that had not been dubbed into English, so they were not well known to other American Anime enthusiasts. One day, while watching a Japanese language movie subtitled in English, he observed a characters regularly rattling off long tirades, but the subtitles said simple things like, "Let's go!" Paul was convinced he was missing out. He made it his mission to discover what was really said.

Like any Millennial, Paul hopped on the Internet and looked for ways to learn Japanese. As he explored Japanese, what really caught his attention was the written language. Japanese consists of three writing systems. Two, Hiragana and Katakana, are phonetically based. The third, Kanji, uses pictographs taken from Chinese. Many find Eastern languages to be mysterious and foreboding. Paul found beauty in the mystery. He discovered that websites that avoided providing vocabulary in Japanese script provided only a superficial treatment of the language. Soon, he was spending five to six hours daily exploring sites that taught how to read Japanese in order to gain a deeper understanding. He even started his own website to help others who wanted to start learning Japanese.

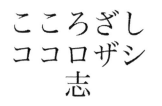

The Hiragana, Katakana, and Kanji forms for Japanese word "kokorozashi" (ambition)

What parent would object to their college freshman child enthusiastically studying a foreign language? The only problem was that Paul was not enrolled in Japanese—he was enrolled in Spanish. While he managed to maintain his grades in other classes, he failed Spanish.

Paul reassessed his values. He realized he had allowed the pleasure with Anime to take priority over his value of education. He also realized that he valued language and helping people unlock the mysteries of Japanese. Paul understood that as useful as Spanish *could* be in his day-to-day affairs, he had a passion for Japanese and became ambitious about helping others learn it. He became a Japanese Studies major in college and studied a semester in Japan. His enthusiasm drove his fluency, which allowed him to attend regular classes with Japanese students. He even took a basic Chinese class in Japan to give himself another perspective on the language. He also taught English classes in the community where he was staying.

Paul's overseas experience reinforced his ambition to help others acquire language skills, and he pursued a Master's Degree in Education so that he could learn advanced ideas for developing a curriculum to teach others.

Paul is especially fond of Kanji, the pictographic part of Japanese. He loves the concept that the pictures can represent words or whole thoughts. Pursuing his ambition, Paul is developing methods for teaching people strategies to unlock the secrets of the pictures, even if they have not seen a particular Kanji character before. He is truly working to make a picture worth a thousand words.

Failing Spanish did not make Paul a failure; it helped him clarify his values. Pursuing a passion has helped him develop an ambition that allows him to live his values. When we understand our values and declare our ambitions for our lives, we will encounter purpose and joy.

Chapter 13: What You Value Gets Done
Defining and Expressing Your Value System and Ambitions

There is so much to do, and so little time to do it in. With so many things that we *could* be doing, how do we choose? Let me ask you, what *is* really important to you?

Why do we seem to have so many distractions in our lives?

There are many things competing for our time and attention. If we are going to get anything meaningful accomplished—the things we truly care about—we have to filter out the distractions and focus on the choices that are truly important.

We have the same 24 hours a day. People that succeed at the highest levels have figured out what is truly important to them. They have well-developed value systems (or "values"). They also have long-range ambitions, informed by their values, which keep them relentlessly laser-focused to the exclusion of everything else.

Values to Guide Us. Our value systems are the collection of principles, beliefs, people and/or things each of us holds most important in life. For example, America was founded on the values of freedom and individual liberty. Our values inform our decisions and guide our actions.

The graphic on the next page shows the relationship between our values and the action-oriented versions of our values: Ambitions, Goals, and Priorities. While we often think about goals and priorities, many people never think about the larger and longer term desires they might have. I call these your *Ambitions*. An ambition is a long-term objective that you want to achieve. It has many of the characteristics of a goal. Ambitions are more open-ended, but have enough clarity to create the emotional connection necessary to see them through to achievement. While a goal might have major phases or milestones, an ambition has major projects or goals that help define it and make it specific.

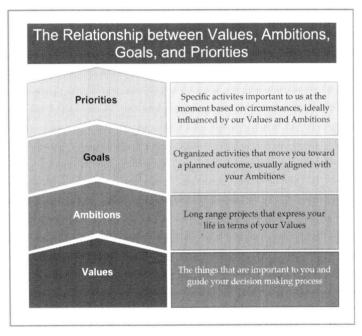

The Relationship between Values, Ambitions, Goals, and Priorities

Priorities — Specific activites important to us at the moment based on circumstances, ideally influenced by our Values and Ambitions

Goals — Organized activities that move you toward a planned outcome, usually aligned with your Ambitions

Ambitions — Long range projects that express your life in terms of your Values

Values — The things that are important to you and guide your decision making process

Our values are always competing with each other for attention. Which values should be given priority in your life will depend upon the purpose we assign to our lives, which is often expressed in terms of our ambitions. Each of us has ambitions to do certain things, not simply to achieve them, but because they meet particular needs in our lives. When we align our ambitions and our values, we discover the clear path forward that helps us decide what we should be doing.

Darren Hardy, publisher of *Success Magazine* related a story of a major corporation that wanted Sir Richard Branson, head of the Virgin corporate empire, as the keynote speaker at their corporate retreat. They contacted his office and offered $250,000 to have him come speak for a half a day—and they were politely refused. No explanation; just refused. Thinking that Branson was playing hard to get, they upped their offer to $500,000, and then $1,000,000. Still, they were refused. The CEO was not to be deterred, however. He wanted one of the most successful men on the planet to speak to his people. He finally asked Branson to name his price.

Sir Richard's personal secretary replied, thanking the CEO for the compliment. She explained, however, that while Sir Richard realizes there are many people who would love to spend time with him, and would probably even benefit from the engagement, that he has certain goals and objectives for himself and his organization that he is working on at present. He is so focused on them that he refuses invitations outside of those priorities, regardless of the price.

Sir Richard clearly understands his priorities, knows his ambitions, and is committed to achieving them. This ability is one of the reasons he has become one of the most accomplished men of our time.

Ambitions in Life. When it comes to accomplishing your own goals, you may have heard, "focus on the big things, and the little things will take care of themselves." At the same time, however, "the devil's in the details." Which of these views is right?

Branson would argue that there is no contradiction between these statements. The first concerns the subject of our work, while the second focuses on executing the tasks to get the work done. With over 400 companies in the Virgin conglomerate, Branson knows exactly which details he needs to focus on in order to provide leadership and guidance.

You want to have a rewarding life, so you need to have a clear picture of what you want and you must know how you are making progress. Your ambitions provide the what. Your goals and their tasks are the details that you must track to achieve your ambition. Conditions and priorities change. Do they affect your ambitions or goals? Correctly distinguishing between these is critical if you are going to accomplish things that are meaningful to you.

Understanding our values and the role they play in our decision making process is the key to creating alignment between our ambitions and goals. Our values are like the stars and constellations. They can be used to navigate to our chosen destination. The seasons and our location on the globe affect which constellations we can see and which stars can guide us. Which values are paramount in our lives depends upon where we are and the season of life.

In his book *The 7 Habits of Highly Effective People,* Stephen Covey discussed the difference between leaders and managers. He wrote that managers are focused on execution, making sure the team performs in the most efficient way possible to achieve a bottom line result. Leaders, on the other hand, are focused on whether the team is doing the right things; whether they are moving in a direction that achieves the desired final outcome. In other words, leaders are the navigators, steering the team to the right place. Managers are the people making sure the team works properly so that it can get to the right place.

If you are going to achieve your ambitions and goals, you have to be your own leader and manager. This often creates tension between "Am I doing the right things?" and "Am I doing things right?" Nobody wants to waste time or resources. The solution is to go beyond your goals and examine your priorities. Ambitions give people a context in which they can decide whether their current goals and tasks are helping them get what we really want or are distracting them from their larger plans.

> *Understanding our values and the role they play in our decisions is the key to creating alignment between our ambitions and goals.*

Ambitions are a yardstick we can use to measure the challenges and opportunities we encounter as we work to accomplish them. They help us understand, in a larger sense, whether we are working on the right things. Ambitions help us filter things, people, and circumstances that arise. Without them, many people never achieve their goals. It is a paradox, but without a larger plan—a specific ambition—many people slow down or stop working on the goal they have because they don't want to be without a goal to work on. This makes discovering and clarifying our ambitions critical. The way to ensure that our ambitions are right is to get clear about what we value, casting our values in the context of your purpose in life.

Discovering your purpose in life is exciting. While some seem to have known their purpose for as long as they can remember, most people are unsure how to determine theirs. Clues to your purpose can be found in your values, passions, skills, and ambitions. When you align your purpose and your values—and only work on the things that align with them—you can achieve powerful results. The good news is that you don't have to fully know or understand your purpose to get moving. Taking action with the tools you have at hand will help you discover your purpose in the end.

While helping a client define his ambitions and purpose, his employer lost a contract and he was laid off. When asked about how he was feeling, he said he wasn't sure, but that perhaps he needed to put his ambitions on a back burner and simply look for work.

He did not like the idea of abandoning his ambitions, but he saw no way forward for the moment. I encouraged him to think about the impact having a good job would have on his ambitions. For all but one of them, his job would make a difference—often in the speed or ability to achieve those ambitions. He realized that setting a goal to get a new job was very compatible with his ambitions, and that making it his top goal was not inconsistent. In fact, it helped him to clarify the type job he should seek for his next position.

Defining our ambitions helps us focus and puts our goals into context. Aligning our ambitions and values provides us the means to navigate the opportunities and distractions we will encounter. This helps us to work with confidence, knowing that we are doing the things that really matter in our lives.

Chapter 14: Finding Your Diamonds
How to Clarify Your Values and Ambitions

In his speech *Acres of Diamonds*, Russell Conwell, founder of Temple University, shared the idea that great riches exist in the things we already have. We have to discover those riches and make them our own. Discovering our values and defining our ambitions unlocks for us the riches in our lives.

People value many things, but not all of their values have equal importance to them. This is demonstrated daily in the choices people make. Here are some examples of decisions we make every day based on our values:

- Choosing the kind of food to eat.
- Choosing whom to meet.
- Choosing whether or not to participate in some particular social activity.

Each of these involves weighing several values and acting on that decision. The challenge is to figure out which values are truly important and learning to faithfully and consciously follow through on those choices.

Values, Ambition, and Universal Law. How do you consciously decide which of the myriad principles, beliefs, people, or things that you value should receive permission to rule your life? I believe because the universe operates with established laws, and that there is objective truth. I teach my clients that when we understand and embrace these laws we can mold the universe to create what we want. Fighting these laws makes success difficult, or even impossible. As Conwell suggests in

Acres of Diamonds, we have to discover these truths inside ourselves in order to use them. Your understanding of these truths may evolve with time, just as your understanding of mathematics evolved from arithmetic to algebra and beyond. Math did not change, you did.

There is an Indian story about blind men encountering an elephant for the first time. The men surrounded the elephant but were only able to touch one part of the animal. Their opinion about what an elephant was varied from a tree trunk to a wall to a snake. All were correct in their specific comparison, but none had the big picture or understood much about elephants. When you embark on the journey to find your value system, you might feel like those blind men. However, with time, you will have the opportunity through experience and reflection to expand and refine your values consistent with your growth.

When considering your values, you should reflect on what is really important to you. You should also consider what is true, right, and just. Yes, you could choose to have a corrupt value system. It might bring you short-term pleasure. But your success will eventually collapse under the effort to maintain it contrary to universal law. Your intuition knows what is right and what is right for you now. You can ignore the sensation, but you experience it all the same. Trust your intuition.

In the last chapter we compared a value system to the stars and constellations. While all the stars exist regardless of where we are on Earth or the time of day, our ability to see the stars will vary by location and season. No star is perpetually and universally visible from all places and at all times. The same is true for values. Where we are and where we seek to go will instruct us on the stars we use. For example, while we all value recreation, the person who has earned their fortune and is retiring will make recreation a higher value than someone seeking their fortune. If the second does not place industry above recreation, he might never be able to enjoy the recreational options of the first.

Ambitions are expressions of needs people want to address in their lives. When we meet Jean Valjean, the main character of Victor Hugo's *Les Misérables*, he is a recently released convict whose ambition is to meet his most basic needs. When Valjean avoids arrest for stealing because of the kindly Bishop Myriel, he is given more than enough to satisfy his immediate needs. With the surplus, he turns his life around and his ambitions focus on higher needs including acceptance, creativity, and justice. Until someone's lower order needs, food, shelter, etc., are met, it is hard to aspire to something more significant.

> *Our values and ambitions provide a map and means to navigate the distractions and opportunities that come our way.*

To accomplish something significant, you need to know what you want to do and why you are doing it, as well as have the ambition, or drive, to get it done. People with significant accomplishments get beyond satisfying their every immediate desire and focus on what they really want. Often, these immediate desires are distractions that cause people to focus inward on lower order needs without consideration for their ambitions.

The daily distractions and challenges to our value systems can seem difficult to overcome if we have just begun to clarify our values and ambitions. When people working on weight control compromise their diet with a quick fast food meal after a late night at work, they can excuse themselves for an isolated situation. If this scene is repeated regularly, however, they need to plan so that they do not have to compromise. Regularly compromising values causes anxiety and fear. The anxiety leads to self-criticism. Because people don't like criticizing themselves, they avoid thinking about the situation. As a consequence, they lose focus on their values, creating a growing spiral of guilt, recrimination, and avoidance.

To avoid this problem treat your ambitions like your goals. You need to regularly review them along with your goals and actively involve them in your decision making process. You will see how this works in Part 4.

The principles of planning for your ambitions are similar to those of regular goal setting. Our ambitions express our intention to achieve a purpose while living our values at some point in time. Our ambitions are similar to goals. They are specific enough to create the emotional attachment needed to seem them completed. However, because of their very large nature or long duration, they are somewhat more open-ended than our goals. We can still approach them from a SMART (Specific, Measurable, Achievable, Relevant, and Timely) perspective. When our ambitions are vague and general, it is difficult to keep them on track in the long run.

Your Values and Ambitions vs. Other People's Plans. Are you choosing your life, or are others choosing for you? The answer is not as obvious as you think. For example, why are you working at your current job? Is it simply for the paycheck, or does it fit into a higher category of values and priorities?

My friend and former colleague Anton Quist is a perfect example of this distinction. When I first met Anton, he was a National Champion cyclist. A true amateur athlete, he worked as an independent contractor for the management consulting company I had just joined. He was a skilled software engineer, but his passion was cycling. Software engineering financed his elite cycling activities. He was an expert at delivering more in 35 hours than most software engineers could deliver in 50. Why? He knew his values and ambitions.

Anton has a philosophy that you can only tackle 2½ really big things well at any given time: two things to seriously pursue and one that is more of a hobby. At the time, Anton's priorities were his cycling and work. His social life was important, but not on the same level. One day, we discussed his plans and I showed him how working as an employee of our company could provide him with stability, security, even sponsorship, while he continued to work toward a possible slot on the 2008 Olympic team. I showed him how our plans could work together so that he could have the security of full-time employment, medical insurance, etc., and still pursue his agenda. While he narrowly missed the Olympics, he did compete internationally, representing America at the World Games in 2008.

Anton's dream, however, was to follow his father's footsteps and become a doctor. Recognizing that the time was right as he was finishing his racing career, and having prepared during his time as a software engineer, Anton pursued his new ambition. He was accepted into medical school in 2009. Medical school is no walk in the park, but with the focus of an elite athlete, Anton graduated in 2013. Today, he is a medical doctor and a member of the Board of Directors of USA Cycling.

Our values and ambitions provide a map and means to navigate the distractions and opportunities that come our way. With clear values and ambitions, it becomes easier to see when opportunities to work with others will help everyone to advance their goals.

SAVE THE HONEY BEES!

 EARTHJUSTICE

SAVE THE HONEY BEES!

EARTHJUSTICE

Chapter 15: Turning Ideas into Action - Values and Ambitions

Exercises to Align Your Values, Ambitions, and Goals

Are you clear about your values? Your ambitions? The two exercises in this chapter will start you on the journey to clearly articulating both. The first exercise will help you identify which of your core values are most important to you. The second exercise will help you identify and clarify your ambitions. If you have not already, you can download the worksheets at 5SecretsOfGoalSetting.com/Resources. You can also find the worksheet at the end of the chapter.

Establishing Your Core Values

Have you ever thought about your value system? Do you know which values are most important to you? If not, let's get started. If you have, congratulations! You are on your way to navigating toward your ambitions. You might want to complete the exercise to confirm your thinking, or simply use the form to record the ones that are most important to you. And if you have not thought about your values before, you are in for a treat. When you are clear about your values and focus on them as you make decisions, you will begin to get powerful results.

This exercise uses a three-step process to develop your goals, as shown in the graphic on the next page.

I recommend that you work quickly to complete the exercise. You will use the output to help you with the exercise on ambitions, which will help you determine if you have targeted the right core values. Review the exercise in a week to see how you feel about it—perhaps redoing the exercise after you have given your subconscious mind a chance to really work on the challenge. Let's get started.

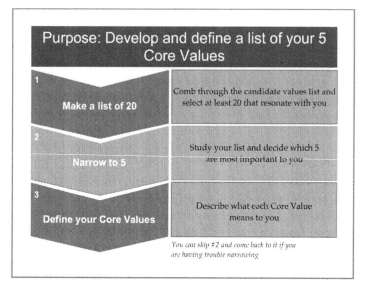

Purpose: Develop and define a list of your 5 Core Values

1 Make a list of 20	Comb through the candidate values list and select at least 20 that resonate with you
2 Narrow to 5	Study your list and decide which 5 are most important to you
3 Define your Core Values	Describe what each Core Value means to you

You can skip #2 and come back to it if you are having trouble narrowing

1. Candidate List of Values. The first page of the worksheet identifies over 150 candidate values. Most are single words. They are intended to stimulate your thinking. I am not saying that a single word should be your goal. While you might settle on a longer phrase, being able to use a single word to describe your values is handy. West Point's values, *Duty, Honor, Country,* clearly indicate the character of that institution. The point of this list is to stimulate your thinking.

Take a few minutes to read the list. Circle or highlight ones that appeal to you. If you don't see something there you think is a candidate value, just jot it down at the end. Your goal is to identify at least 20 things that represent principles, ideas, people, and/or things you value in your life.

Work quickly. You will likely find many things that you

value. Only pick those that really jump out at you as something about which you feel strongly. Your ultimate goal is to find the MOST important ones for you, so start narrowing now.

2. Narrow the List. Once you have your first pass list, study it and pick the five values most important to you. Trust your intuition. If that doesn't work for you, prune ones you know are not as important until you get the list down to five. Some of my clients struggle with this approach. If that is you, then skip to step 3, and try this again when you finish it.

3. Describe Your Core Values. Now describe what each of the selected values means to you. The words or phrases you chose could mean just about anything to anybody, but they mean something specific to you. Write out these meanings.

Personally, I like short, simple core value lists because they are easy to remember. I like to think of the descriptions as the definitions of the values. The descriptions are useful when sharing values with others, especially when you are working on projects together.

If you find it hard to narrow your list to your most important values before writing the descriptions, just go ahead and write our meanings for all the values you think are important to you. Ultimately, I encourage clients to develop a list of their important values, a group that expands the core values to a list of 10 to 20. Creating descriptions for all of your candidate core values can help you clarify all of your most important values.

Declaring Your Ambitions

What are the big things you want to get done? Are they really important to you?

Our Core Values focus on the types of things that are important to us. Ambitions are programs we pursue to live our values to their fullest. This means that our ambitions should align with our values. Have you ever thought about what your ambitions are? If not, this exercise will help you declare your ambition by understanding how the goals you are currently pursuing suggest something larger than those goals themselves. The graphic illustrates the steps.

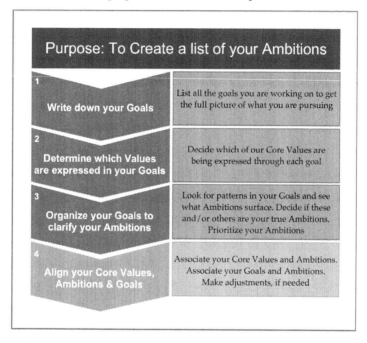

1. Write Down Your Goals. If you are reading this book, I would guess that you are a person who wants to get important things done. That means that you already have some goals you want to accomplish. In the first table of the second worksheet, write down all of the goals you are working on right now, or plan to begin in the near future. (Have you developed Goal worksheets for each? If not, why not go back to the exercise in Chapter 4 and complete one for each?)

2. Determine Which Values Are Expressed in Each Goal. Take a moment and think about your goals and your Core Values. For each goal: how do your Core Values guide you in its pursuit? Which values are being expressed in each? Jot the core values down next to each goal they influence. What if you have goals that are not associated with your core values? For the moment, continue to the next step. We will explore this issue a little later in the process.

3. Organize Your Goals to Clarify Your Ambitions. If you want to be a high achiever like Sir Richard Branson or Dr. Anton Quist, you have to focus intensely on your ambitions. Begin by studying your goal list.

- Are there long-term goals that fully express your values?
- Are there themes that run through your goal list?

These are candidate ambitions for your life. Consider how your goals work together and identify two to five major ambitions for you to focus on over the next one to five years. Why this spread? Dr. Quist's rule was 2½. His ambitions were large and very long term. The larger and longer range your ambitions, the fewer you should have in order to keep focused on them. Here is an example: Say that your goals are:

- Climb the highest peak on each continent
- Write a book about climbing Mt. Everest
- Open a school for mountain climbing

Your ambition might be to be a world-class mountain climber. Or it could be to become one of the world's leading authorities on mountain climbing. How might you tell the difference? Opening the school and writing the book might be goals to help you raise money for your activities. However, if one of your Core Values is teaching others about the majesty of the mountains, then perhaps you really want to be an authority. Neither choice is better or worse, except in how it relates to your values.

Finish writing out your ambitions on the second table and associate your Core Values with your ambitions. Now study the list carefully. Which of your ambitions is most important to you? Go ahead and assign a rank order to your ambitions.

Why do you need a rank order when these are the most important things for you to be working on? Dr. Quist found he could not manage more than a couple of things at once. He put his ambition to be a doctor on hold because he realized that medical school required the same level of commitment as elite cycling. He chose to pursue the more physical one while he was younger, saving medical school for after his cycling career. When you understand which ambitions have a higher priority, you can see where one ambition is becoming a distraction for another and adjust your activities accordingly. If you find that your circumstances have changed the ranking among your ambitions, you are free to change them and readjust your activities.

4. Align your Ambitions, Values, and Goals. Go back to your goal list and associate your goals with your ambitions, if you can. Naturally, because of the way we did this exercise, some of your goals might be ambitions unto themselves. Remove them from the goal list. Look at the rest: do they align with your ambitions? If they do, assign the applicable ambition's ranking in the third column.

Study the goals that do not support any ambition. Ask yourself why did you set those goals? Do they really connect to a current ambition, or are they something to defer until other things are accomplished?

Now look closely at your goals and ambitions and consider your values. If you have properly selected your core values and ambitions, each priority should have one or more Core Values associated with it. Goals that are associated with an ambition can be associated with that ambition's values, even if the goal does not relate to a Core Value. Sometimes we have to do things that in themselves might not seem important, but are important to larger things.

If on the other hand, you have ambitions or unassociated goals that do not link to Core Values, it should be a warning flag to you. If this is your first time doing this exercise, it could mean that you have not correctly identified your Core Values. It could also mean that the goal or ambition is not as important to you as you think. Consider what you should do. Maybe you need to reconsider your values. Maybe you need to delegate a goal or defer an ambition. The choice is yours.

When you finish, you will have a list of goals and priorities you can be confident will help you express your values and achieve your dreams.

Establishing Your Core Values

- Pick 20 candidate values from this list, or jot down your own at the end.
- Work quickly. You will know immediately if it is something that is a strong value.
- Narrow the 20 the 5 most important to you and transfer them to the chart on the next page

Abundance	Comfort	Encourage
Acceptance	Compassion	Endow
Accomplishment	Community	Energy
Achievement	Composure	Enlist
Adaptability	Confidence	Environmentalism
Add value	Connection	Excellence
Advancement	Contentment	Expectancy
Affluence	Control	Experiment
Alertness	Coolness	Explain
Anticipation	Courage	Extravagance
Approval	Creativity	Facilitate
Assurance	Daring	Fame
Audacity	Deference	Family
Awe	Determination	Fashion
Being the best	Diligence	Ferocity
Bliss	Discernment	Financial
Brilliance	Discretion	independence
Calmness	Dreaming	Flexibility
Capability	Dynamism	Fluency
Celebrity	Economy	Foster
Change	Education	Freedom
Cheerfulness	Elation	Friendship
Cleverness	Empathize	Gallantry

A: Achieving Alignment

Gentility

Grant

Gregariousness

Happiness

Heart

Hedonism

Holiness

Honor

Hospitality

Hygiene

Impartiality

Individuality

Inform

Insightfulness

Instruct

Intelligence

Intrepidness

Intuitiveness

Involvement

Justice

Leadership

Lightness

Love

Marriage

Mastery

Meekness

Mental

Mindfulness

Modesty

Moral

Mysteriousness

Nonconformity

Open-mindedness

Organization

Outrageousness

Patience

Perfection

Philanthropy

Physical

Pleasure

Potency

Precision

Preparedness

Pride

Proactivity

Provide

Purity

Rationality

Recreation

Relaxation

Resilience

Respect

Reverence

Rules

Sacrifice

Score

See

Self-respect

Sensitivity

Sensuality

Service

Silence

Sincerity

Solitude

Spark

Spirit

Sports

Status

Stimulate

Structure

Supremacy

Synergy

Temperance

Thoroughness

Thrill

Touch

Triumph

Truth

Uniqueness

Valor

Virtue

Vision

Volunteering

Willingness

World Peace

Youthfulness

Zeal

Room for your ideas

State Your Core Values

Value	Description

Declaring Your Ambitions

Linking Goals and Values

Goal	Values	Ambition

5 Secrets of Goal Setting

Defining Your Ambitions

Ambition	Values	Ranking

Chapter 16: Review - Achieving Alignment
Key Points about Values and Ambitions

- We have Values, Ambitions, Goals, and Priorities to guide our activities
    - o **Values** are the things that are important to you and guide your decision making process
    - o **Ambitions** are the long-range projects that express your life in terms of your values
    - o **Goals** are organized activities that move you toward a planned outcome, usually aligned with your Ambitions
    - o **Priorities** are specific activities important to us at the moment based on circumstances, ideally influenced by our Values and Ambitions.

- Our values and ambitions provide a map and means to navigate the distractions and opportunities that come our way.

- Our ambitions express our intention to achieve a purpose while living our values at a point in time.

- Linking our goals with our ambitions helps us understand how important a goal is to us.

- Our priorities are linked to our values, whether or not we are consciously aware of the connection.

- Achieving alignment happens as we explicitly link our values and ambitions.

- Alignment helps us avoid distractions.

- If your Core Values, Ambitions, and Goals do not align, you need to consider why and make adjustments accordingly.

- If you do not decide your own ambitions, you risk being made part of other people's plans with no long-term benefit to yourself.

- Understanding our values and the role they play in our decision making process is the key to creating alignment between our ambitions and goals.

Part 4—L: Learning and Adjusting

"Your success is based upon your daily habits and agenda."
—John C. Maxwell

G: Getting Great Goals

O: Overcoming You

A: Achieving Alignment

L: Learning and Adjusting

S: Staying the Course

Chapter 17: Learning or Entertaining?

How a World Class Leader Keeps Growing

Many people are willing to work hard to achieve their goals. But for some reason, people are much more interested in working hard than checking to see if they are really making progress. Perhaps they have heard stories of athletes looking over their shoulders just as they are reaching the finish line and losing to others still looking ahead. Was "review" really the problem? These athletes made two mistakes. First, they were reviewing at an inappropriate time. Second, they were checking the progress of others instead of focusing on their own. These athletes wanted to succeed. What they needed to do was find the right time and the right things to review.

One attribute of a good goal we learned in Part 1 was that they are *measurable*. If you do not bother to take time periodically to measure your progress, it could actually cost you time in the long run. Review allows us to learn and adjust our plans to better fit the situation, our experience, and our needs. Through review, we can see patterns that could be slowing us down and correct them. We might also see patterns that could allow us to double or triple our productivity while saving time and energy. Review also provides us with ideas and techniques we can use in later projects, allowing us to achieve our ambitions in better, more fulfilling ways than we could have imagined when we embraced them. Let me share with you the story of one of my mentors and how review has made a difference in his life.

Internationally acclaimed leadership expert Dr. John C. Maxwell is the son of a scholar. Family life for John and his siblings was a little bit different than most of us experienced growing up. Chores were expected of all family members as their dues for being part of the family, so the children were not paid to do them. The children's work was to learn, so John's parents paid them to read books.

One day, after having finished another book, John's father asked him a question: "What did you get from your reading today?" John was caught off-guard. His father explained to him that if he didn't take the time to capture what he learned from reading, he wasn't really learning—he was simply being entertained.

How many of us are entertaining ourselves when, with just a little additional effort, we could be educating ourselves?

John saw his father's point. To act on his father's advice, John built 4 daily habits that he continues to this day. Daily, he started:

- *Reading* things that helped him grow,
- *Thinking* about what he read,
- *Writing* about what he'd read and thought about, and
- *Filing* what he wrote so that he could access it later and put it to use.

This has created an archive for John—50 years' worth of notes—that he uses constantly to get ideas and inspiration for the books he has written, over 60 to date, and the speeches that he gives around the world.

John's daily habit of reading, thinking, writing, and filing led him to wonder how he could go beyond simple awareness and turn what he was learning into action. From that desire he created a methodology he calls ACT that he applies to the things he learns, and which you will learn to use in Chapter 19.

As a result of John's consistent habits, his desire to learn, and his application of the lessons he's learned, he grew to become a very successful Christian pastor, leading one of the top 10 largest congregations in America before moving on to become an internationally-known expert on the subject of leadership.

A simple habit of reviewing what he'd done during the day helped John take entertaining things he discovered and turn them into practical actions that have benefitted him and the world. Reviewing what we do on a regular basis can provide us the tools and inspiration to live our own lives of significance.

Chapter 18: We Measure What We Value

Reviewing Our Progress towards Our Goals

How do we know whether or not we really value something? We evaluate it. Good or bad, we evaluate every aspect of things we value. Concerned parents carefully watch their children grow. They encourage them when they make mistakes and discipline them when they misbehave. Why? They want the best for their children. Golfers are looking for the new club or video that will deal with their hook or slice, trimming a few strokes from their score. Woodworkers subscribe to magazines to learn about the latest techniques to save them time and effort. Artists enter shows in order to have their work judged, and so that they can get inspiration to do more and better.

We also evaluate things to determine whether or not they are worthy of our continued time and investment. For example, we look at "sell by" and "use by" dates on food. Sports fans are constantly reviewing team and individual statistics, especially if they are in a fantasy football league. They evaluate their players' strengths and weaknesses to determine what they might need to do in order to win the league championship.

Reviewing is the intentional act of looking back on recent activities in order to compare them to our plans and measures so that we can measure their effectiveness and our progress. We need to know what progress we are making. We also need to take a moment and identify potential risks and opportunities. Review helps us maintain focus on the things that are really important, ensuring that we are getting the job done.

Socrates told his students "the greatest good of a man is daily to converse about virtue." By virtue, he is talking about the things that are valuable and important to us. We want to constantly study the things that are important; if we're not examining them, then life becomes very shallow. For, as he also said, "the unexamined life is not worth living."

Roadblocks to Review. If review is so important, why don't people do more of it? The two biggest barriers to regular review are setting unrealistic goals and our innate human aversion to being evaluated. Before I understood how to set good goals, I avoided reviewing. Half the time I was setting unrealistic goals and then criticizing myself for not achieving them. People don't want to be judged and found wanting.

I found myself spending more time wondering what is wrong with me, rather than resetting a more realistic goal. That's what we

> *If you want to achieve meaningful goals, review is critical to your success.*

do—looking inward and criticizing ourselves, instead of focusing on the problem at hand. Achieving a goal is a long-term endeavor. Not all of the activities we plan in the process of obtaining our goal will work out the way we want. If we are taking action toward our goals, mistakes and failures along the way are necessary so that you can find the true path forward.

The third major barrier to review is over-reviewing. Often when people start regular reviews, they spend more time than they need reviewing. Based on your goals, you need to determine how much and how often you should review.

When I first started reviewing, I had no idea how to conduct any sort of review. As a consequence, I spent two hours a day reviewing the day's activities. I would write detailed diary entries, cataloging what I did, what others thought, problems, solutions, etc. While I found it fun and insightful, eventually I started to avoid this time-consuming activity. I started to procrastinate because it seemed that there were better ways to spend my time. Actually, after a while, I abandoned reviewing because I was falling into barrier #1 and criticizing myself for not reviewing more often.

Eventually, someone recommended I read *How I Raised Myself from Failure to Success in Selling*. Author Frank Bettger (pronounced "bet-cher") described his weekly review process. He examined every aspect of each sales call and prospecting activity to learn lessons from his successes and failures. Over the course of two years, he improved his productivity, becoming the top salesman in his company, while cutting his workweek to four days.

If you want to achieve meaningful goals, review is critical to your success. If you are working multiple significant goals, you will need to review regularly: daily, weekly, and monthly. When you consistently review, you will see powerful results.

Chapter 19: A Conversation with Yourself

The Anatomy of a Review

Determining the right level and frequency of review is an exercise in balance. We strike that balance by remembering why we are reviewing and remembering what is essential to the type review we are doing.

Broken into its parts, a review involves three activities:

- Examining
- Evaluating
- Planning

Examining is the process of studying the use of time and resources in support of the goal. You should look at your appointments, scheduled tasks, unscheduled activities, and unplanned activities. Your goal is to understand what you did and why you did it.

Evaluating is judging the effectiveness of the activities examined. You created ways to measure your goals; in this step you will apply them to see if your results are matching your expectations. During this stage, you will also examine deviations to understand their underlying cause. Evaluation is also a time to capture lessons learned.

Planning is determining what needs to be done now to continue progress toward the goal. In the previous two stages, you considered what had been done, why it was done, and whether it was satisfying your needs. Now you need to decide what you will be doing next. Planning can be as simple as affirming that you will continue according to plan. It can also involve reassessing plans in light of new information, risks, or situations.

One thing I learned managing large software projects is that being ahead of schedule and under budget is neither good nor bad on its own. You have to consider the context of the variance. When we review, we need to examine variances in our plans to determine root causes and decide what, if anything, we need to do. For example, if your plan is under budget, it might mean that you forgot to make a critical purchase. Being ahead of schedule could be the work of an innovative new approach, or it could mean that work did not meet quality standards.

The Steinway & Sons Corporation takes a year to build a concert grand piano. Surprisingly, much of that time the piano is sitting in place with no real work going on. The reason they do this is because the process of creating a grand piano puts a lot of the parts under stress as the wood is shaped and the strings are put under tension. The piano is tuned at least 5 times during that year, to different degrees and standards that put the necessary strain on all the parts to work out any imperfections. All this, so that when the piano is ready to be sold it will have the highest quality sound and reliably stay in tune.

ACT-ing on Lessons Learned. It is also important to document lessons learned as you move along. Many organizations pay lip service to lessons learned, but only bother capturing them after the end of a project. They miss opportunities that could have saved them time, effort, and money because their review was incomplete. There might be things we could learn from our review sessions that would help our personal development or benefit others.

One strategy for documenting lessons learned is a method

that John Maxwell calls ACT:

- **Apply:** something new that you could apply to your life
- **Change:** an idea or strategy for doing something differently
- **Teach:** something that would benefit others to know

The first step is to identify possible ACTs. As you review, if you see something you might want to apply to your life, put an "A" next to it. If the thing is something you need to change, then put down a "C". If it is something you could teach others, put a "T."

Sometimes these ACTs will be things critical to the success of your goal. Handle those accordingly. Most things, however, are not urgent. Rather, they are fertile ideas that *could* be done. Some might be distractions. It is easy to become so enthusiastic about your ACTs that they distract you from your goals. Therefore, simply collect the ACTs and review them monthly. Examine all your As, Cs, and Ts, and pick one of each that you can act on for the next few months.

Only one? What about all those other great observations?

The first month after I learned about ACT, I had collected over 500 ACTs. Had I tried to act on all of them, I would have become very un-focused and lost sight of my goals and ambitions. Picking just one in each area keeps you learning and growing, but also keeps you focused. Taking your time and deciding carefully what new ideas you will tackle allows you time to consider which are really important to you and align with your current priorities.

The Right Amount of Review. How often should you review? I recommend you review daily, weekly, monthly, and annually. A quarterly review could be good, too, but I leave that up to you. The key is not so much the intervals as picking the right things to do at each interval. In Chapter 20, you will get specific recommendations for developing daily, weekly, and monthly reviews. These principles can be applied to quarterly and annual reviews as well. The key is to create a fertile environment where you are eager to study your goals and continue to make progress toward their achievement.

Chapter 20: Turning Ideas into Action – Reviewing

Exercises in Reviewing

Are you ready to start reviewing? The exercises below are full of great questions that will help you bring your activities into focus at an appropriate level at an appropriate interval, so that you can make everything effective.

The worksheets are at 5SecretsOfGoalSetting.com/Resources.

The Strategy for Reviewing

Reviews are part of a planning and monitoring cycle; so all reviewing begins by considering the plans you have developed for your goals. Be sure you have completed Goal worksheets for your key goals so that you can keep your goals in front of you. The graphic on the next page depicts a strategy for reviewing.

1. Find a time to review. You want to be sure you have broken your goals down into enough detail that you can work on them. For many of my clients working on their personal goals, we use a monthly window as the primary timeframe. However, more complex goals might require longer windows. The key is to decide the major things you need do in those timeframes (i.e., each month) until your goal is achieved.

With the general plan developed, as you come into each month, you want to do your major planning for a month all at once. Usually this means reviewing what you did in the past month, studying what you previously planned to do for the coming month, and decide what you really will do, taking into account circumstances and what you learned from your review. Do not just establish general parameters for the month. Get specific. Decide what should get done each week in the month. If some of the work requires making appointments or scheduling specific work times because of team or resource availability, make plans for specific days.

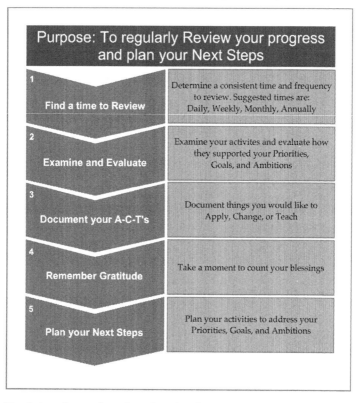

Purpose: To regularly Review your progress and plan your Next Steps	
1 Find a time to Review	Determine a consistent time and frequency to review. Suggested times are: Daily, Weekly, Monthly, Annually
2 Examine and Evaluate	Examine your activites and evaluate how they supported your Priorities, Goals, and Ambitions
3 Document your A-C-T's	Document things you would like to Apply, Change, or Teach
4 Remember Gratitude	Take a moment to count your blessings
5 Plan your Next Steps	Plan your activities to address your Priorities, Goals, and Ambitions

By doing the major planning for the month in advance, your weekly reviews can focus on progress week to week, and making adjustments to plan based on circumstances. You will be looking for trends during the week, which makes this a great time to evaluate whether you are procrastinating over anything. Daily reviews are used to make sure you stay focused and committed to your goals. Daily planning then focuses on ensuring that the plan for the next day is clear so that you can remain focused on making progress.

2. Examine and Evaluate. The structure for your reviews should focus on the Examining, Evaluating, Planning model, recognizing that Examining and Evaluating are often done in tandem. The questions in the worksheet provide a framework to guide you through the process if you have limited experience. Feel free to expand the questions to meet your needs.

3. Document your A-C-Ts. As the questions suggest, think about the lessons you are learning as you review. Ask yourself if there are things you might want to Apply or Change in your life, or Teach others. Note them so that they do not become a distraction. In your monthly review, consider which A-C-Ts you actually want to implement.

4. Remember Gratitude. A sense of gratitude will help you take action, even when you are feeling stuck. Don't forget to include it as you examine, evaluate, and plan.

5. Plan your next steps. Complete the Examine, Evaluate, Plan process by planning your next steps, consistent with your level of review. This completes the strategy discussed in Step 1. Armed with your plan, continue taking action!

Questions for Daily Review

- What were my intentions for the day? What did I think would be important? Did I do it?

- Did I make time to consider my ambitions today? Did I act on them?

- Was I prepared for my appointments? What was the outcome?

- What did I do on my "To Do" List? What did I do on my "To Don't" List?

- How did I use my unscheduled time?

- What am I grateful for today?

- What is planned for tomorrow? What appointments? What tasks?

- What can I do to work on my ambitions tomorrow?

L: Learning and Adjusting

Questions for Weekly Review

- What trends do I see in the preparation, presentation, and outcomes of my appointments?

- How did my appointments and tasks performed this week support my ambitions?

- How was my use of unscheduled time? Was I committed to completing planned tasks?

- What distractions did I allow to take my time this week? What activities triggered those actions? What can I do to control my environment to avoid those distractions?

- How well did this week's activities support my goals for the month? What adjustments do I need to make?

- What were my A-C-Ts this week?

- What am I grateful for this week?

- What is the most important task to accomplish next week? Does this support my goals and ambitions?

- Where can I schedule time to commit to each of my ambitions next week?

- What does my weekly schedule need to look like next week so that I can make progress toward my goals and ambitions?

Questions for Monthly Review

- What victories did I have this month? Where did I come up short?

- How have I been making progress on my goals? My ambitions? Do I need to adjust the plans?

- Are my goals supporting my ambitions? How committed am I to my ambitions?

- What is my calendar telling me about my values, my use of time, and my ambitions?

- What do I need to do each week next month to keep on track toward achieving my goals and accomplishing my ambitions?

- What am I grateful for this month?

- Which A-C-Ts do I want to embrace for the coming month?

- What other Physical, Mental, Spiritual, Social, and Financial activities should I focus on next month?

Chapter 21: Review - Learning and Adjusting

Key Points about Reviewing

- We value what we measure.

- Examining our goals and our lives helps us stay focused on our ambitions, and ensures we get our work done.

- Review does not have to be a burdensome thing.

- A review session consists of:

  o **Examining** what was done
  o **Evaluating** work against plans and standards
  o **Planning** for the next period

- Capture your lessons learned with the **ACT** methodology:

  o **Apply:** something you don't do now that you want to add to your life
  o **Change:** something you would like to do differently in your life
  o **Teach:** something you want to share with others in your life

- Regular review should happen daily, weekly, monthly, and annually.

- If you don't take the time to capture what you learn from reading, you are not really learning—you are simply being entertained.

- Reviewing what we do on a regular basis provides us

with the tools and inspiration to live our own lives of significance.

- Reviewing is the intentional act of looking back on recent activities in order to compare them to our plans and measures so that we can measure their effectiveness and our progress.

- If you want to achieve meaningful goals, review is critical to your success.

- Daily reviews are used to make sure you stay focused and committed to your goals.

Part 5—S: Staying the Course

"I hated every minute of training, but I said, 'Don't quit! Suffer now, and live the rest of your life as a champion!'"
—Muhammad Ali

G: Getting Great Goals

O: Overcoming You

A: Achieving Alignment

L: Learning and Adjusting

S: Staying the Course

Chapter 22: You're Gonna Get Wet

Pursuing a Dream—Even when You Must Get Wet Once in a While

Getting started is necessary to achieve any goal. Equally important is staying the course. We must be persistent and take consistent ACTION in order to achieve our goals. Are you really willing to persist against all obstacles until you achieve your goals? Have you had people, family, and friends laugh at your goal? Have you ever had to dive into the ocean to retrieve a soccer ball that has gone out of bounds? Let me share with you the story of an unusual football club.

There are fishing villages in Thailand that exist on the edge of the world. Built on platforms extending off the shore and into the sea, fishermen live and ply their trade there because of land ownership laws and the naturally rugged terrain.

Koh Panyee is one such village, just off the shore of Thailand. In the 1980s it was a thriving community that had all of the normal things you would expect in a community—except for open space. While the people were not exactly rich, they had creature comforts such as television, radio, and children. But they had no parks or playgrounds.

One of the things the boys of Koh Panyee loved doing was watching football (soccer, here in America). As much as they enjoyed the game, however, the constraints of their village sticking out over the water meant that there was no place for them to play the game.

As football fever swept the island again during the 1986

121

World Cup, a group of boys asked themselves could they create their own place to play. Many of their elders laughed—no land meant no "pitch" (soccer field, in America). But the boys were undeterred. They gathered scrap wood and old fishing rafts, using them to create a flat, dock-like structure that became their pitch.

> *Getting started is necessary to achieve any goal. Equally important is staying the course.*

It wasn't particularly large—about a quarter of the size of a football pitch—but it gave the boys a place to enjoy the game. That's not to say that they didn't have challenges, however. Out-of-bounds balls meant going into the water to retrieve them. Wood gets slippery when wet. Further, used wood has hazards such as splinters and nails that periodically work themselves loose.

In spite of these challenges, the boys had a great time. Living their dream, they started to think bigger: "How good are we compared to others?" When word came that there would be a tournament on the mainland, they excitedly signed up.

The boys' commitment and desire had not gone unnoticed by their elders. They were amazed to see how the boys turned their dream into something the village had imagined was impossible. Like the boys, they were curious to see how far the team could go. To show their support, they purchased uniforms for the boys as a reward celebrating this major milestone.

The Koh Panyee team surprised people at the tournament. Coming up through the brackets, they regularly outperformed their opponents. Their unique practice environment had forced them to develop strong skills in areas such as ball handling and passing. Practicing with goals a quarter of regulation size made their shots on goal more accurate.

Going into the championship game, they faced a very talented team. At the end of the first half, Koh Panyee was down two goals. It started to rain quite hard during that game, and the boys weren't used to playing in shoes—much less wet ones.

At halftime, deciding they had nothing to lose, they removed their cleats and played the rest of the game barefoot, the way they did at home. They rediscovered their ability to fight and win, and they took back those two points, tying the score.

Unfortunately, a last minute goal cost them the game. Yet, they still achieved something incredible. Untried and untested, they had entered a major regional tournament and they finished in second place. Their performance unified their village and inspired others. Their amazing accomplishment helped them to find sponsors to improve their facilities, which generated an excitement on the team that created a winning tradition at Koh Panyee that includes several Thai national championships.

The boys of Koh Panyee had a dream. They weren't even sure how to achieve it when they first started; they just knew that they wanted to be great football players, like those they saw playing in the World Cup. By persisting in spite of the challenges and the limitations that were placed before them, they succeeded beyond their expectations—making a difference in their own lives, their village, Thailand, and the world.

You don't need a world-class ambition to make a difference in the world. The dreams you have can be enough to start the journey.

Chapter 23: The Second Star to the Right and Straight on 'til Morning

Staying the Course and Celebrating Along the Way

Setting and achieving goals often works like a trip to Neverland in Peter Pan. We get excited about the prospect that we can fly, and we can't wait to head out to the second star on the right to find the adventure awaiting underneath. What we don't count on is dealing with the unknown traveling in the dark of night. Challenges and uncertainties can make the night a lonely time. Naturally, once we're at Neverland, there's a whole new set of opportunities and challenges—there are fun things, but there are very real dangers as well. In the end, we leave Neverland because we realize that we can dream bigger dreams and achieve even more in the real world.

We like the idea of achieving our goals and arriving at a destination. However, the trip itself can get very tedious. As a kid growing up in San Jose, California the beaches of Santa Cruz were just over an hour away. Being at the beach was a great time, but I dreaded beach days. It wasn't being at the beach that I hated. It was the idea of sitting in the car in traffic, bored and not in control. It also didn't help matters that I got carsick occasionally, either.

Anything worthwhile requires commitment. We don't need commitment when things are fun and exciting. We need it when the long hours of tedium necessary to complete the unglamorous parts of our goal challenge our will to continue.

We don't achieve our goals simply because we start the journey, although it is necessary. We achieve our goals because we take action, follow through, and complete the process.

Achieving our goals requires persistence. The key to persistence is action. Taking action and completing the individual steps in our plans creates enthusiasm, making it easier to maintain a positive mental attitude. We must constantly fight that little voice that wants to say, "Is it really worth it? Does it really matter? Can I really do it?" "Will it work for me?"

Reminding yourself of why you are on the journey is critical to maintaining your efforts. That is one reason why in the 5-Step Goal Setting Process you created a detailed vision of your success. It's also why you need to read it daily. By keeping your reason why in front of you, you create an emotional need to achieve it. Like Muhammad Ali, you make the choice to live like a champion by getting through the challenges that are immediately in front of you on a day-to-day basis.

> *We achieve our goals because we take action, follow through, and complete the process.*

All worthwhile goals take time to achieve. They require you to act consistently over time. Life is going to challenge you as you work on your goals. Sometimes, you have to struggle to find time to get things done. When I was running a management consulting practice, one of the challenges I regularly faced was dealing with the emergencies that kept cropping up and getting in the way of the work that only I could do.

Review helps you avoid being trapped doing things that aren't working. It also helps you distinguish between distractions and opportunities that can accelerate your progress.

Even when things are busy, however, it is critical that you

find some time for your goals. Little actions taken daily make a difference. Even if you only have five or ten minutes a day to work on your goals, that will help you stay consistent and eventually achieve them. Action focuses you on the outcomes you want to have, keeping you motivated to continue to work and get things done.

Smelling the Roses along the Way. It is also important that you remember to celebrate the victories along the way. Many people that think the only time they can celebrate is when something is totally done—often calling it "delayed gratification". I support the concept of delayed gratification in its proper context, waiting to get something until you have completed a plan to get it. But delayed gratification does not mean that you have to give up any possibility of reward or recognition before achieving your ultimate goal.

If your goal is saving $100,000 in the bank, it does not make sense to throw a $5,000 party in celebration of the fact that you have $25,000. You would be sending yourself backwards a significant amount. You could use a little of that money to reward yourself, however. Perhaps you can do something more modest, such as a nice dinner.

Celebration does not have to be out of proportion with what has been accomplished, but celebrations are an important opportunity to recognize progress and create excitement for the next phase of the task—especially when you are working with a team. Celebration is a form of gratitude, and can help motivate your team to action.

Often, there are team members that are not fully connected with the team's plans and progress. It is critical that all are aware of accomplishments, and that their efforts are appreciated. Each member of your team has a preferred way of receiving feedback; for maximum effect it's important to accommodate this where reasonable. For example, some people appreciate a personal expression, such as an aside or a note. Others appreciate being recognized in front of others.

Celebrating and recognizing people for what they are doing is what is going to get them excited. It will turn the completion of that phase into the start of the next trip to Neverland for you and your team, recreating that "I'm just getting started" excitement of pursuing a new goal.

To stay the course, we must continue to act on our plans for our goals, even when our work becomes monotonous and tedious. Keeping our goals in front of us and regularly reviewing are critical to maintaining enthusiasm. Remembering to celebrate the small victories along the way gives us perspective and a taste of the great things to come when we achieve our goals.

Chapter 24: Turning Obstacles into Opportunities

What to Do When Your Belief is Challenged

The biggest challenge to perseverance is discouragement. When you are discouraged you wonder if you are doing anything valuable and whether you should continue. Discouragement comes primarily from three sources:

- **Boredom.** Tedium makes people wonder if the reward is worth the effort. This has been discussed thoroughly, especially in Chapter 8 on procrastination.

- **Distractions.** Life gets in the way, sometimes. People can get so busy addressing assorted crises that they lose sight of what they need to do to achieve their goals. They may feel guilty that they have left something incomplete and have not returned to finish it. Often they waste time judging themselves in these situations. Instead, they should focus on re-establishing alignment with their ambitions and start moving again.

- **Inertia.** The tendency for things to continue as they are is inertia. When things are moving smoothly, we don't worry about it because we have momentum. Inertia is working for us. But when things come to a halt because of failure or the unintended consequences of previous actions, inertia is an enemy. It causes people to lose focus, creating confusion and stress.

In Chapter 9, you were asked if you approach problems from

the perspective of "What is this going to do to me?" or "What is the opportunity in this?" To move ahead you have to think about the opportunities being presented to you.

How can you find something good when you're having problems?

Glass manufacturer Corning provides an example. In the 1950s, one of their scientists put an experimental glass sample in an oven. He was supposed to heat the oven to 600°C, pull out the sample, and let it go through a process to cool and anneal the sample. There was

> *When faced with a challenge, think about what opportunity lies within this problem and you will find new and unexpected ways to achieve your goals.*

a malfunction with the oven's temperature gauges, and the sample was heated to 900°C. The scientist was concerned that the malfunction would ruin both the sample and the oven, because glass can explode when it gets overheated.

Instead of an ugly mess, however, the sample was a puddle of white liquid that was remarkably tough when cooled. The new glass was 10 times stronger than most regular types of glass then available, making it nearly as strong as steel. This made it very durable under a lot of circumstances—including providing shatter protection when the glass was subjected to sharp impacts.

Corning immediately recognized that they were onto something, and introduced a product line that became a must-have fashion accessory of a 1960s kitchen called Corningware—the ubiquitous white glass cooking and serving pieces with blue cornflowers stenciled into the glass.

The story could have ended there, but Corning realized that

glass as strong as steel had to have other applications. Eventually, they devised a clear version. Corning offered it for windshields, replacing laminated safety glass. Unfortunately, in crash tests, the test dummy skulls were fractured because they were not as strong as the windshield. Automobile manufacturers were not keen to have a windshield that was going to break heads instead of saving lives.

Corning shelved the product, reviewing it occasionally, but nothing emerged until Steve Jobs approached Corning CEO Wendell Weeks trying to find a glass that could be manufactured 1.3 millimeters thick and have an incredibly high break resistance—four to five times what was then available in regular glass. Weeks knew exactly what Jobs needed. The catch was that Apple wanted delivery in six months.

Weeks was not deterred. In 8 weeks Corning provided samples that met Apple's requirement, allowing them to continue. Four months later, Gorilla Glass debuted on the iPhone. Today, Gorilla Glass accounts for a major share of the screens on handheld and tablet computing devices, and is also finding new applications daily in larger-scale devices, including televisions and computer monitors.

So remember: when faced with a challenge, think about what the opportunity is that lies in this problem and you will find new and unexpected ways to achieve your goals and make your dreams come true.

Chapter 25: Turning Ideas into Action – Persistence

An Exercise to Help You Find a Way Forward

The three major challenges to persistence are boredom, distractions, and inertia. Dealing with boredom and distractions were addressed in Part 2, so our exercise in persistence is going to look at how to turn problems into opportunities.

The worksheets are at 5SecretsOfGoalSetting.com/Resources.

Purpose: To find your way forward when stuck

1 Understand the situation	Describe the situation. What is slowing you down?
2 Identify influencing issues	Write down the things, good or bad, that influence the current situation
3 Determine the Key Element	What one thing, if addressed, would put the situation back on track?
4 Develop plan to get moving	Determine the action steps that will address the Key Element
5 Take ACTION	Carry out your plan

How do you know that inertia has set in? You are dealing with inertia when you are struggling to move forward, frustrated because you know you are not procrastinating. In physics, force must be used to break inertia. The graphic on the next page shows the steps you must take to break inertia.

1. Understand the Situation. In the first block, briefly describe your situation. What is slowing you down?

2. Identify the Influencing Issues. Next, consider what things are influencing the situation. These might be constraints such as budget or regulations, decision makers, the weather, etc., depending upon your situation. Figure out what they are and then ask yourself, "What is the influence?" Is it real or valid? Sometimes we assume things to be limiting our options, but the limit is our assumption, not the thing itself.

3. Determine the Key Element. Now that you understand your situation and the influences, determine the one thing that, if addressed, would put the situation back on track. Notice that I did not say to "solve the problem." Your goal is to get back into action so that you can turn inertia into your friend. Staying still trying to solve the problem does not get you back into action. As you look for the key that would get the situation moving again, you may find the solution to the situation. Great! Treat it as a bonus and get moving!

4. Develop a Plan. Once you understand what will get the situation back on track, determine what action steps are needed. The form has space for four steps, which is often plenty to get into action. If you need a few more, determine them.

5. Take ACTION. Now that you have thought through your challenge and determined a way to start moving forward, take that action and turn inertia into your friend.

Focus on Action

What is the situation?	
What are the influencing factors, good and bad?	
What is the key element that, if addressed, would put the situation on track?	
List the Action Steps that Focus on addressing the key element	
Action Step 1	
Action Step 2	
Action Step 3	
Action Step 4	

Chapter 26: Review - Staying the Course
Key Points about Persistence

- All worthwhile goals require sustained effort to achieve.

- Getting started is necessary to achieve any goal. Equally important is staying the course.

- Persistence tests our true values over the long term, showing us what we truly put first.

- Being persistent becomes much easier when you know your destination, and can envision what awaits you when you arrive.

- Celebrating victories along the way reminds you that you are achieving progress, and reminds your team of their progress as well.

- Celebrations can also be the springboard to a rededication and renewal of the energy and excitement of getting the job done.

- We don't achieve our goals simply because we start the journey, although it is necessary. We achieve our goals because we take action, follow through, and complete the process.

- By keeping your reason why in front of you, you create an emotional need to achieve it.

- When faced with a challenge, think about what the opportunity is that lies in this problem and you will find new and unexpected ways to achieve your goals.

Epilogue

The Book is Finished, but Your Journey Has Just Begun

As you can see setting goals will get you started toward the life you always wanted to have. Focused Action is the key to staying the course. The process begins with GOALS:

G: **Getting Great Goals.** Having goals so that you have a plan you are pursuing to get what you want.

O: **Overcoming Yourself.** Beating fear and procrastination through action, eliminating your tolerations, and remembering to express gratitude.

A: **Achieving Alignment.** Discovering your Core Values and living them fully by pursuing your Ambitions.

L: **Learning and Adjusting.** Regularly reviewing your activities to discover and apply lessons learned, accelerating your progress.

S: **Staying the Course.** Committing to the action needed to see your goals to achievement, and enjoying the journey and rewards along the way.

At the end of *Willy Wonka and the Chocolate Factory*, Mr. Wonka looks at Charlie and says, "Don't forget what happened to the man who suddenly got everything he always wanted. He lived happily ever after." Some might think this a curse, what could somebody possibly do now? But if you think about it, having everything you always wanted does not mean that there are no more important things to do. Maybe doing something significant *is* what you always wanted. My wish for you is that you get everything you always wanted. I hope that you will discover your true values and ambitions so that you get on the path to living exactly the life you want.

Next Steps and Support

How to Stay Connected with the 5 Secrets Team

5 Secrets of Goal Setting is an introduction to the whole field of personal development and achievement. I hope that you will continue your journey so that you can have everything you want. To help you, I encourage you to continue your progress. I have some resources that can help you:

- **5SecretsOfGoalSetting.com.** You have probably already visited the website to download copies of the worksheets that accompany the book. Our blog will provide weekly tips and stories relating to the GOALS methodology.

- **Webinars.** Are you interested in learning to apply the suggestions from 5 Secrets of Goal Setting? I will be offering periodic webinars about putting the 5 Secrets to work. The first two will be January 14, 2014. Check 5SecretsOfGoalSetting.com/Resources for details and additional dates.

Do you have a success story about using the 5 Secrets of Goal Setting? Please send me a note at

success@5SecretsOfGoalSetting.com

I might even share it on the blog to inspire others.

Special Offers for *5 Secrets of Goal Setting* Readers

5 Secrets of Goal Setting Workbook

Ready to put what you just read into action? *The 5 Secrets of Goal Setting Workbook* is the companion you need to get the most from *5 Secrets of Goal Setting*. In addition to full-size, writable versions of the forms found in this volume, the workbook contains additional tips and tricks designed to help you get the most from the activities as you go along.

If you want to move beyond setting goals and into achieving them, this workbook is an indispensable partner to help you go the distance. Used properly, the forms provided will provide an excellent way to chart your progress and share your dreams with others, as well.

The 5 Secrets of Goal Setting Workbook is available now at http://www.5SecretsOfGoalSetting.com/GetBook.

Goal Achievement Boot Camp

Are you looking to take still more action on your goals? Do you want to develop the discipline to be able to know that something will get done once you decide to do it?

Goal Achievement Boot Camp is a four-week program that digs deep into the mechanics of taking action on your goals. Your cadre will meet for 30 minutes daily via teleconference to learn skills and help each other be accountable to follow through on the actions needed to successfully plan and achieve our goals. Topics to be covered include:

- Personal Accountability
- Goal Setting
- Focus
- Creativity
- Purpose

- Power of the Mind
- Achievement Mindset
- Reviewing Techniques
- The Power of Today
- Breaking Barriers

How it works: Odd numbered sessions introduce techniques and provide homework. Even numbered sessions focus on questions and accountability. The whole program is designed to make it easy to learn and act on new habits.

Over the course of the program, you will:

- Define, plan, and begin execution on the goals most important to you
- Learn 10 strategies to help you keep focus and follow through with your goals
- Develop confidence that you can achieve even your biggest dreams

Sign up today and develop the discipline you need to achieve more in the next 12 months than you ever have before. Go to either http://5SecretsOfGoalSetting.com/Events or http://dbaptist.com/mastermind for dates and tuition.

Use discount code 5secretsdeal and receive $100 off tuition (limit 1 discount per tuition).

No Success is Too Small

Are you frustrated and feel as though it does not matter what you do, you will never succeed? Are your goals looming large over you, mocking you so that you feel as though you are a failure, a fraud?

Many people think that they cannot be a success unless they accomplish really big goals. They are taught "delayed gratification" or "self-denial" until they reach those goals. Frustrated, they give up on their goals and indulge themselves in the things they have been denying themselves, feeling guilty and like a failure.

No Success is Too Small by Dwayne and Ellen Baptist provides a fresh perspective on work, ambition, and success. Through stories and exercises, Dwayne and Ellen will show that you are not a failure, and show you how to celebrate your accomplishments big and small. Through stories and exercises, you will be guided through a process to clarify your passions, ambitions, and values so that you can get focused on your most important goal, building in smaller milestones—places to review, reflect, and celebrate the progress.

Using our past successes as inspiration and focusing our passions, values, and skills to do little things every day we can discover our purpose and achieve great things.

No Success is Too Small will be available in print and for Kindle March 1, 2014. Check http://www.kokorozashipress.com/NotTooSmall for purchase and distribution information.

The Gratitude Journal

Documenting what you are grateful for unlocks a lot of potential in your life in a number of ways:

- It reminds us of the good things that are happening to us daily
- It helps us to keep perspective when things are not well, and to see a brighter future
- It calls to mind who has helped us along our journey, and that we need to thank them
- It inspires us to act as a response to the graciousness and generosity we received through our blessings

Sprinkled with wit and wisdom *The Gratitude Journal* provides space to document your blessings for a whole year. The Gratitude Journal provides inspiration, exercises, and tips demonstrating the power of gratitude.

The Gratitude Journal will be available for sale March 1, 2014. Check http://www.kokorozashipress.com/NotTooSmall for purchase and distribution information.

The Gratitude Journal makes a great gift for springtime occasions, including Easter, Mother's Day, or as a sendoff for your favorite graduate.

Together Inspiring Personal Success

Do you have something you want to change or achieve in your life? Maybe you'd like to...

- start a business
- find new love
- get a raise
- lose weight
- get your children to behave better
- or something else

No matter what you'd like to change or achieve, the secrets to success are the same:

Define. You have to decide *exactly* what you want and develop a burning desire to have it. Clarity and a burning desire are critical components of goal achievement.

Become. You will have to change to get what you really want. You will have to develop new skills and abilities, expand your circle of acquaintances, and shed limiting behaviors and beliefs so that you can be the person who can accomplish your goals.

Achieve. You must take focused action to get to your goals, but you do not have to act alone. Few achieve great things alone. Star athletes have teammates and coaches to help them, and fans to perform for. Finding people to help and support your Focused Action improves your chance for success.

Together Inspiring Personal Success (TIPS) is a program that brings people together to experience personal growth. TIPS provides a safe environment to establish goals, get equipped, and find support as you take focused action to achieve your goals. Meeting weekly via teleconference, TIPS members participate in a personal development program while also working on their personal goals in a positive environment.

Join TIPS this summer and get:

- Tools to clarify your goals and develop a burning desire to achieve them
- A personal development system to shed the limiting habits and beliefs that are holding you back, and develop the skills and habits you need to succeed
- Accountability to keep you focused and avoid distractions
- A team to inspire you, and maybe even help you achieve your goals

For more information, visit http://successtips.me

Putting the 5 Secrets to Work

Are you interested in putting the 5 Secrets to work in your life? Would you like help getting great goals, reviewing or continuing to take Focused Action? Join Dwayne for a regularly scheduled **Free** webinar providing details that will help you understand and apply the 5 Secrets to:

- Clarify your values and ambitions
- Create a burning desire for accomplishing your goals
- Conduct regular reviews that help you adjust your plans and move ahead
- Conquer fear and procrastination
- Continue towards your goals through Focused Action

For more information and to sign up for this free event visit http://5SecretsOfGoalSetting.com/Events